Elemental Magic
The Hidden Realm of Fairies

Luiz Santos

Copyright © 2023 Luiz Santos
All rights reserved. No part of this book may be reproduced in any form or by any means without written permission from the copyright holder.
Cover image © Vellaz Studio
Review by Armando Vellaz
Graphic design by Sara Mendez
Layout by Humbert Costa
All rights reserved to:
Luiz A. Santos
Category: Holism

Table of Contents

Prologue 5
Chapter 1 Introduction to Fairies 8
Chapter 2 Elemental Energy 15
Chapter 3 Spiritual Connection 22
Chapter 4 Preparation for Rituals 30
Chapter 5 Fairy Invocation 36
Chapter 6 Healing Ritual 42
Chapter 7 Protection Ritual 49
Chapter 8 Prosperity Ritual 56
Chapter 9 Alignment with Nature 64
Chapter 10 Advanced Energy Work 71
Chapter 11 Sharing Wisdom 79
Chapter 12 Energy Awareness 87
Chapter 13 Renewal Rituals 94
Chapter 14 Self-Love Ritual 101
Chapter 15 Communication with Nature 107
Chapter 16 Alignment with Natural Cycles 114
Chapter 17 Practices for the Community 122
Chapter 18 Inner Wisdom Ritual 129
Chapter 19 Caring for the Altar 136
Chapter 20 Advanced Spiritual Protection 143

Chapter 21 Self-Knowledge and Growth 149
Chapter 22 Manifestation Practices 156
Chapter 23 Deep Emotional Healing 162
Chapter 24 Working with Elementals 167
Chapter 25 Deep Purification Ritual 173
Chapter 26 Developing Intuition 179
Chapter 27 Harmony in Relationships... 184
Chapter 28 Deepening Practice 190
Chapter 29 Ancestry and Fairies 196
Chapter 30 Self-Healing Ritual 203
Chapter 31 Final Consecration 209
Epilogue.. 215

Prologue

You are about to enter a rare, somewhat intangible world—a universe pulsing at the borders of the visible and the hidden, where the ordinary becomes extraordinary. This book is not just a read; it is a passage, a key that opens doors to a dimension where fairies dwell, where the primal forces of earth, water, fire, and air whisper ancient secrets that resonate at the very core of your being. And this invitation is for you alone, as if each line, each word, were written to awaken something slumbering yet essential within you.

At first, it may feel like you are simply turning pages, but soon you'll realize you're opening portals. This is a unique calling, a journey offered only to those who dare to look beyond the surface and ask what truly exists beyond the boundaries of what we consider "real." This book does not aim to explain but to reveal. The fairies that dance across its pages are not ethereal beings from childhood tales but guardians of an ancient harmony, a wisdom that binds the human to the divine, the spiritual to the physical.

Picture yourself beside them, learning to listen to the earth, feeling the flow of the waters, sensing the warmth of the fire, and soaring with the air. Fairies are more than characters; they are living forces, energies that permeate nature itself, embodying each element in its purest, most transformative form. They are also guardians, silent observers who, for millennia, have maintained order among nature's realms. By connecting with them, you also tune into this balance, reassessing your role in the eternal dance of life and renewal.

Each chapter will guide you deeper into this realm of mystery, where hidden truths begin to emerge subtly, like a soft light filtering through morning mist. As you read, let yourself be drawn into this atmosphere, allowing yourself to go beyond the words, feeling in every phrase the energy these beings carry. Realize that in unveiling the mysteries of fairies, you are also discovering hidden parts of yourself. By touching nature, you will also touch your essence—an essence inextricably linked to this very world.

The fairies of the elements—earth, water, fire, and air—mirror the deep qualities that reside within you. Earth fairies, with their quiet, grounding energy, invite you to reconnect with stability, with what is solid and enduring. They are the guardians of nurturing forces, of growth and sustenance, and by connecting with these energies, you will discover a calm and steady strength that nurtures your spirit.

Water fairies, meanwhile, guide your emotions, bringing lightness to the experience of adapting, receiving, and releasing. They swim in deep waters, in the ocean of emotions, dreams, and instincts, helping you understand that true freedom lies in allowing yourself to be fluid and adaptable, just like a current flowing around obstacles, constantly renewing itself. With this presence, you will learn that the fluidity of water is a force in itself and that introspection is a tool for renewal.

Fire fairies, intense and transformative, are the guardians of creative power. They challenge the ordinary and inspire change, urging us to seek transformation and rebirth. You cannot connect with them without feeling your own creative potential awaken, without sensing that inner spark ready to ignite new ideas, to burn away what no longer serves you, and make room for the new. They not only bring warmth but also light, inviting you to look within and see your truths with clarity.

And then there are the air fairies, mysterious and ethereal presences that bring the lightness and clarity of thought. They move in the space between thoughts, between dreams and visions, inspiring new ideas and encouraging mental freedom. These fairies allow us to elevate our thinking, to let go of burdens and constraints, and to float freely within possibilities. By connecting with the energy of air, you will learn to release what limits you and open yourself to the power of imagination and intuition, allowing thought to travel beyond what is concrete and immediate.

As you open yourself to this universe, allow your own sensitivity to awaken to the signs of the unseen. Like nature itself, fairies reveal themselves only to those who are willing to observe, to listen, and to harmonize. This reading is more than a book; it is a guide to a subtle transformation, to a new way of perceiving yourself and the world. With every page you turn, you will draw closer to this portal of knowledge that transcends the rational, to a knowing that connects body and spirit to the very essence of nature.

This book invites you, therefore, to rediscover the energies that compose your own soul, energies mirrored by the elements around you. It challenges you to reconnect, to realize that by aligning yourself with these forces, you participate in a greater dance, in a flow that interweaves all forms of life. And, in the end, you will find that this dance leads you to a point of beginning—a place where the ordinary and the extraordinary coexist, where you and nature are one, where harmony and mystery reside in perfect synchrony.

Chapter 1
Introduction to Fairies

In the hidden realms where light meets shadow and the whispering trees sway with secrets, there exists a world of ethereal beings—known to many as fairies. These elusive creatures are more than mere tales passed down through ancient lore. They are elemental beings, woven from the very fabric of nature itself, embodying the primal energies that sustain our world. To glimpse a fairy, or even sense their presence, is to encounter an essence as old as the earth, as fluid as water, as warm as fire, and as free as the wind. Here, in the folds of reality that often go unnoticed, fairies dwell.

The fairies' existence speaks to a profound balance within nature. Each one aligns with a specific element—earth, water, fire, or air—reflecting its unique qualities and energies. Yet, fairies are not solely manifestations of these forces; they also serve as their guardians, protectors of the delicate equilibrium that underpins the natural world. In this role, they act almost as a bridge, a connective thread between the human and elemental realms, watching over the life that flourishes within the ecosystems of which they are an intrinsic part.

Different types of fairies arise within these elements, each carrying distinct energies, appearances, and purposes. Earth fairies, for instance, are drawn to stones, roots, and the deep, quiet places within forests. Often linked with growth and stability, these beings resonate with energies that ground and nurture, working silently beneath our feet to foster life. The earth-bound fairies find sanctuary within the trees and soil, where they guide the cycles of growth and decay, whispering to the plants and fauna in a language beyond human hearing.

The water fairies, on the other hand, flow with the rivers, lakes, and seas, their essence tied to the ebb and flow of water, and by extension, to our emotions. To connect with water fairies is to touch the ever-changing rhythm of feelings, memory, and intuition. They swirl within the currents, shimmering as playful reflections on the water's surface or as fleeting movements beneath its depths. Their purpose is to inspire cleansing, renewal, and adaptability, for they are the breath of fluidity in nature, adapting to every curve and current they encounter.

Fire fairies carry an entirely different energy. Known for their intensity, they flicker within flames and the warmth of the sun, radiating a vibrant life force that commands attention. They embody transformation, urging the world to embrace change and move through cycles of rebirth. While their energy can seem fierce, fire fairies possess an intricate wisdom—one that teaches us to respect the power of passion, will, and renewal. When these fairies appear, their presence often reminds us to harness our inner fire, to channel courage, and to seek illumination within ourselves.

And then there are the air fairies, the most elusive of all, flitting invisibly through the skies. They are the bearers of inspiration, messengers of clarity and insight, who inhabit the spaces between thoughts and dreams. These fairies are drawn to open fields, mountaintops, and the gentle rustling of leaves, where their airy essence can dance freely. They breathe life into ideas, often appearing as moments of sudden clarity or a gentle breeze that brings a whisper of intuition. The presence of air fairies invites us to elevate our thoughts, to let go of burdens, and to embrace the power of unseen possibilities.

Together, these elemental fairies create a tapestry of energies that permeates nature. Their roles are as varied as their forms, but they share a unifying purpose: maintaining harmony and fostering growth within the natural world. They are allies of balance, moving through a rhythm that is constant yet ever-evolving, and in their wisdom lies an understanding of the interdependence of all things.

Yet fairies are not merely passive keepers of nature. They are also interactive beings, responsive to those who seek them with respect and open hearts. For those who wish to connect with fairies, it is essential to approach them as one would approach a wise and ancient teacher—without demands, but with reverence and curiosity. Fairies sense intentions, responding to energies and emotions rather than words. They may appear to those who approach them with humility, seeking to learn and harmonize with nature rather than control it. In this way, fairies may choose to reveal themselves subtly, perhaps as a glimmer of light in the corner of one's vision, a gentle breeze carrying a scent of flowers, or even a fleeting melody that stirs a long-forgotten memory.

Understanding the fairies is, therefore, a journey of spiritual alignment. It requires attuning oneself to the natural world, becoming aware of the subtle currents and unseen forces that shape it. Fairies exist within these unseen realms, woven into the energies that fill forests, rivers, fires, and skies. By learning to perceive these energies, one begins to glimpse the fairy world—a place both within and beyond the boundaries of our physical reality.

As we open ourselves to this realm, we may find that the fairies teach us as much about ourselves as they do about nature. They mirror the qualities of our own inner elements, guiding us to connect with the earth, water, fire, and air within. In doing so, fairies remind us of our place within the larger tapestry of life. They reveal that we are not separate from nature but are, in fact, an integral part of its essence—a truth that we often overlook.

This initial exploration of the fairy realm offers a glimpse into a mystical reality where energy, intention, and respect blend. Fairies, as elemental beings, embody and sustain the natural forces around us, harmonizing with the spirit of the world in a dance of energy and life. To understand them is to embark on a journey of spiritual alignment, one that leads us closer to the heart of nature and, ultimately, to the hidden aspects of ourselves.

When one dares to deepen their understanding of fairies, the path unfolds like a tapestry, woven with threads of perception and energy that are as delicate as they are profound. To walk among fairies is to learn their language—not through words, but through an intuitive dance of feeling and intention. Each fairy type brings its own rhythm, communicating in whispers and signs rather than concrete forms, opening a window into the subtler layers of existence.

The earth fairies, silent keepers of growth and decay, echo with the heartbeat of the land. They do not speak in audible tones but rather in shifts and sensations: a growing warmth, a sense of grounding, or a subtle vibration felt in the stillness of ancient trees. To perceive their presence, one must listen not with the ears but with the spirit, tuning into the slow, steady pulse that beats below one's feet. When humans enter their sanctuaries—the moss-covered stones, hidden groves, or the gentle rolling of hills—there may be a sense of calm, a feeling of being watched by something both ancient and wise. Earth fairies communicate through the essence of patience, nurturing the seeds of growth within both nature and the soul.

Water fairies, in contrast, are creatures of fluidity, aligned with the tides and flows of our inner emotions. They appear in reflections, darting beneath the surface or shimmering as ripples in the calm. These fairies reveal themselves in moments of introspection, helping one navigate the depths of feeling and intuition. Connecting with them invites an embrace of change, for just as water moves and reshapes itself effortlessly, so too do these fairies guide us to flow with life's currents. To sense their presence is to feel a pull, an invitation to delve inward and to move gracefully through one's own emotions, finding clarity in the depths.

The energy of fire fairies, meanwhile, resonates with intensity and transformation. Fierce protectors and keepers of passion, they appear as flashes of light, flickers in a candle's flame, or even in the warmth of a sunlit space. While their energy can be sharp, it is also richly creative, urging those who connect with it to ignite their own inner fire. Fire fairies embody the essence of change, teaching us to release what no longer serves us and embrace our core truths with courage. They respond most vividly to intentions of growth and empowerment, reminding us that transformation begins within. Their presence stirs a feeling of both warmth and vigilance, a reminder to respect the power of fire and use it wisely.

Air fairies, like a gentle breeze carrying the scent of flowers, are the most subtle of all. They reveal themselves through movement, a rustling in the leaves, or a fleeting thought that inspires. Unlike the rooted energy of earth fairies or the passionate flow of fire, air fairies bring a whisper of inspiration, urging us to look beyond the surface of reality. When they are near, one may feel a lightness, a sense of possibility, and an openness that allows new perspectives to drift in. They are messengers of clarity, guiding us to release burdens and tune into the unseen. In their ethereal presence, there is a sense of expansion, a reminder to dream and imagine without restraint.

To interact with fairies of any type, sensitivity and presence are essential. Fairies respond to those who are attentive to the energies of their surroundings. For humans, this often requires a form of unlearning—a loosening of the hold that modern distractions have on our senses. By practicing presence and patience, by walking through nature with an open heart and a clear mind, one can begin to perceive these energies, connecting with the fairies as one would with trusted friends. Fairies see past surface intentions, responding only to the energy and respect offered by those who approach.

For those who feel drawn to the fairy realm, certain practices can help build a bridge between worlds. Meditation, for instance, quiets the mind and attunes it to the subtle, rhythmic energies that signal a fairy's presence. During these moments of stillness, the spiritual senses awaken, revealing the hum of life that often goes unnoticed. Simple practices, like placing a stone or a flower as an offering, express one's reverence and appreciation for nature's delicate balance, inviting fairies to take notice.

In places where fairies are especially active—such as groves, near streams, or under the open sky at twilight—a shift in energy may be felt. With time, one learns to recognize these subtle signs: a sense of being watched, an inexplicable warmth, or the sight of small, darting lights in one's peripheral vision. These moments are invitations to pause, to let go of distractions and listen, sensing the presence that moves just beyond the boundary of sight. The connection becomes not only a bridge to fairies but to the soul's deeper self, a journey inward as much as it is outward.

As humans deepen their connection with fairies, they may also find that nature itself begins to reveal its wisdom. The cycles of growth and rest, the harmony between predator and prey, the rhythm of seasons—these are the principles that fairies uphold. Working with fairies encourages an alignment with these natural rhythms, fostering a life that mirrors the balance they so diligently maintain. In this way, fairy encounters become more than magical experiences; they are lessons in harmony, resilience, and interconnectedness.

Fairies, however, are guardians of a world beyond human understanding. Their perspective is ancient, rooted in a timeless wisdom that sees not only the present moment but the endless cycles of life that connect all things. To them, life is a continuous dance of energy, constantly shifting but never-ending. Those who come to fairies seeking knowledge or assistance find that they are drawn into this dance, learning not through direct instruction but through the lived experience of interacting with these beings.

In this dance, fairies may help illuminate hidden aspects of ourselves. By engaging with them, one begins to see beyond the physical and to trust in intuition and unseen forces. Fairies are not merely symbols or archetypes; they are beings who choose to share their presence and energy, guiding those willing to learn from the mysteries of the natural world.

For those who seek rituals and practices with fairies, understanding these energies lays a vital foundation. The fairy realm offers more than visions or ethereal encounters—it is a reflection of a world where harmony, respect, and connection are paramount. Each fairy type invites humans to align with these principles, to reconnect with nature in a way that feels both timeless and profoundly personal.

In this way, fairies guide us not just toward them but back to ourselves, fostering a journey that is both spiritual and transformative. As the path unfolds, the boundaries between human and fairy, between seen and unseen, blur, revealing a world alive with hidden beauty and wisdom waiting to be discovered.

Chapter 2
Elemental Energy

Within the ancient dance of nature, where every leaf, stone, and breeze carries the silent pulse of life, lies a truth that many have sensed but few truly understand: the presence of elemental energies. These are the forces that animate not only the world of fairies but also the very foundation of existence itself. Like the threads of a vast, invisible web, elemental energies weave through everything, binding each aspect of life to the next. Earth, water, fire, and air—each element a distinct yet inseparable part of the whole—are channels through which fairies manifest and exert their influence, shaping the natural world in ways both subtle and profound.

The earth element embodies solidity, a force of endurance and nourishment that breathes life into trees and anchors the ground beneath our feet. This energy is dense, steady, and unyielding, yet within it pulses the subtle magic of growth and regeneration. Earth fairies are guardians of this power, custodians of all that is rooted, grounded, and stable. They dwell within the fertile soil, sheltering seeds as they journey from germination to full bloom, and in doing so, they act as silent protectors of life's cyclical nature. Those who attune to earth energy often feel a sense of grounding, a calm that draws them closer to their own roots, inspiring patience and a reverence for growth. In the presence of earth fairies, there is a palpable stillness, a reminder that strength lies not in force but in quiet persistence.

The energy of water, ever fluid and adaptive, is both the mirror and muse of our emotions. Water fairies embody this flow, moving in harmony with rivers, lakes, and streams, guiding the gentle rhythms of purification, reflection, and change. They are spirits of intuition, gliding effortlessly between the visible and the hidden, navigating the depths of feeling that so often remain unspoken. To connect with water fairies is to experience a gentle invitation to surrender—to let go of resistance, to flow with life's current, and to embrace each twist and turn with grace. In the movement of water, these fairies remind us of the cleansing power of release, encouraging us to let go of emotional burdens and allow ourselves to feel fully.

Fire, by contrast, radiates intensity, sparking transformation and illuminating the path forward. It is an element of passion, a force that consumes, purifies, and rebirths. Fire fairies dance within flames, their flickering forms alive with a potent energy that urges action and awakens dormant strengths. They are keepers of change, guiding those who call upon them through the fires of personal transformation. To embrace fire energy is to ignite the inner flame, to awaken the courage and drive that propel one's spirit toward its highest aspirations. Fire fairies encourage us to shed what no longer serves, to embrace our passions without fear, and to honor the lessons in destruction and rebirth.

The air element, elusive and omnipresent, is a conduit for inspiration and insight. It is a force that permeates all things yet remains intangible, ever moving and unbound. Air fairies inhabit the spaces between breaths, dancing upon the breezes that stir the mind to clarity and imagination. Their energy is swift and light, opening pathways of thought and communication, guiding us to lift our gaze from the tangible and explore realms of possibility. In moments of sudden insight or creativity, one might feel the touch of an air fairy—a nudge that opens the mind to ideas beyond ordinary perception. They invite us to think expansively, to break free from constraint, and to embrace the freedom of thought and imagination.

Each of these elements, though distinct, is inherently interconnected. Just as earth supports water, water quenches fire, fire rises with air, and air fills the spaces within earth, so too do the energies of the fairies entwine and interweave, creating a harmonious balance that sustains all life. Fairies, as elemental beings, embody this interplay, channeling the forces of nature to maintain equilibrium within the world. They guide and protect, watching over the fragile balance that allows life to flourish. And though they may appear within a particular element, their energies flow fluidly across boundaries, reminding us that all things are linked by invisible currents of energy and purpose.

In sensing these elemental energies, one begins to understand fairies as more than mythical figures; they become a tangible reflection of the elemental forces themselves. When we connect with them, we are connecting to the very essence of earth, water, fire, and air within us. The stillness of earth grounds us, the fluidity of water nourishes our emotions, the intensity of fire awakens our passions, and the lightness of air inspires our thoughts. This understanding fosters a symbiotic relationship, wherein humans and fairies coexist within a shared web of energy, each respecting and supporting the other's role within nature.

To approach elemental fairies is, therefore, an exercise in attunement, a process of harmonizing one's own energy with the energies around. By learning to sense the unique qualities of each element, one can begin to perceive the presence of fairies and understand their teachings. Grounding exercises can foster connection with earth fairies, while meditative practices by rivers or lakes invite the company of water fairies. Fire rituals and candle gazing can draw fire fairies closer, and open-air meditations allow one to feel the swift, refreshing touch of air fairies. Through these practices, we not only invite fairy energies into our lives but also deepen our connection with nature itself, grounding us in the rhythms of the earth, encouraging flow, igniting purpose, and lifting our spirits.

As we open to the elemental energies, we begin to see the fairies' role as guides and guardians of balance within the natural world. Their presence is both subtle and profound, felt as an undercurrent within each element, guiding us to honor the cycles of life, to respect the forces that sustain us, and to find beauty in the delicate, interconnected web that unites all beings. The fairies, through their work within the elements, offer a path to understanding life's mysteries, not through explanation, but through experience. In their silent, constant work, they remind us of our own place within the world's balance, urging us to live with mindfulness and harmony, to nurture and protect, just as they do.

In this exploration of elemental energies, we stand on the threshold of a deeper wisdom—a wisdom not grasped by intellect alone but felt through the heart, through the senses, and through the spirit. The fairies, guardians of earth, water, fire, and air, open the door to a reality that is both ancient and immediate, calling us to a journey where nature itself becomes our teacher, and where we learn, slowly and gently, to align with the very soul of the world.

As one's senses begin to awaken to the gentle currents of elemental energy, the presence of fairies becomes not merely an abstract concept but a tangible, guiding force. Fairies, these guardians and channelers of nature's primal powers, move through their respective elements with an intelligence and sensitivity that both mirrors and transcends human understanding. Their work within each element is delicate yet powerful, forming a subtle network of energies that uphold the equilibrium of all life. To engage with these energies consciously, to sense them and connect, opens a doorway to a more profound relationship with fairies, a bond that allows one to tap into the elemental forces that animate the natural world.

The energies of each element reveal themselves through careful observation and practiced sensitivity, like glimpses of sunlight on a forest floor. The fairies of earth, for example, move quietly, tending to the roots of trees, the soil, and the stones. Through their energy, one may feel a deep sense of grounding, of connecting with the earth's stabilizing rhythm. A practice to attune to their presence begins by physically touching the ground or a tree, allowing oneself to feel its pulse. Closing one's eyes and sinking into this sensation reveals the energy of earth fairies as a gentle hum, a feeling of rootedness that brings stillness to the mind and body alike. In moments of difficulty or uncertainty, this energy offers stability, teaching patience and resilience. In their wisdom, earth fairies remind us of the importance of grounding ourselves, of reconnecting with the rhythms of growth, renewal, and quiet endurance.

Water fairies, meanwhile, bring forth the energy of fluidity and emotion, gliding through rivers, pools, and even the smallest droplets of dew. Their essence is felt as a cooling presence, an invitation to release and flow with the natural course of life. To attune to water fairies, one might sit by a stream or lake, closing their eyes and listening to the flow, matching one's breath to the rhythm of the water. In doing so, one taps into the water fairy's gentle encouragement to allow emotions to move freely, to cleanse and refresh. Water fairies offer guidance in moments of emotional challenge, encouraging individuals to embrace change with acceptance, to wash away old attachments, and to allow new feelings and experiences to enrich the soul. With their touch, one learns the grace of surrender, finding strength in flexibility and resilience.

The fairies of fire, in contrast, embody passion, transformation, and raw energy. They flicker within flames and warm spaces, stirring the spirit and inspiring acts of courage. Their energy can be intense, felt as a quickening of the pulse or a spark of excitement within. To connect with fire fairies, one may perform a simple ritual with a candle or gaze into a campfire, feeling the warmth and observing the lively dance of flames. In these moments, the presence of fire fairies may be sensed as an inner warmth, a reminder of the transformative power of passion and creativity. They inspire action, urging us to step boldly into change and to embrace life's intensity with a fearless heart. Fire fairies remind us that within every ending lies a new beginning, that the energy of transformation is an essential part of growth and creation.

Air fairies, the most elusive of all, move invisibly through the spaces between thoughts, gliding upon breezes and the open skies. They bring clarity and inspiration, clearing the mind and lifting the spirit. One can feel their presence in moments of lightness, when a sudden insight or creative idea appears unbidden, or when a gentle breeze refreshes the senses. A way to attune to air fairies is through breath, by standing in an open field or on a hillside, feeling the wind on the skin and taking deep, mindful breaths. Through these moments, the energy of air fairies fosters a sense of freedom, opening pathways of thought and inviting curiosity and imagination. Their presence is a reminder to release limitations, to expand one's vision, and to allow ideas and dreams to take flight.

Together, these elemental energies form a complete spectrum, a dance of life that fairies oversee and nourish. For those seeking to connect more deeply with fairies, practicing sensitivity to these energies is a vital step, as it builds an attunement that transcends words and brings one into alignment with the rhythms of nature. One way to cultivate this sensitivity is through a practice called "elemental grounding," in which each of the elements is acknowledged and invited into one's presence, one at a time. By sitting quietly, visualizing the energy of each element—earth as grounding, water as flowing, fire as warming, and air as lifting—one learns to feel each energy distinctly and begins to recognize these forces within their environment. This practice creates a harmonious space where fairies feel welcomed, for it demonstrates a reverence for the energies they nurture and protect.

As one's sensitivity deepens, fairies may begin to respond, offering signs of their presence in ways that are as subtle as the energies they embody. Earth fairies might make themselves known through the vibrant life of a plant, a sense of warmth in the soil, or the feeling of being gently held by the land. Water fairies often bring a sparkle to moving water, a sudden peace by a lake or river, or a slight shiver that awakens the senses to the beauty of fluidity and transformation. Fire fairies reveal themselves in moments of inspiration, a flash of insight, or even a wave of warmth felt in cool air. And air fairies come as whispers, as a cooling breeze that clears the mind, or as thoughts that seem to float in effortlessly, bringing fresh perspectives.

As one learns to perceive these signals, rituals with fairies become more than acts of reverence; they become collaborations, moments when human and fairy energies intertwine. Fairies lend their guidance, shaping the energy of the ritual and imbuing it with the strength and wisdom of the elements. With time, rituals shift from structured practices to fluid expressions of connection and gratitude, as fairies show those willing to listen how to work with elemental energies in harmony, embodying the beauty and wisdom of nature's own balance.

The journey of connecting with fairies through elemental energies does not only open the senses to unseen realms; it reawakens a forgotten relationship with the earth, one that reminds us that we are a part of nature's pulse, that we too carry earth, water, fire, and air within us. Through fairies, we learn that harmony with nature is not an external goal but an internal alignment, a process of becoming attuned to the world and to the self in equal measure.

Thus, each step in this journey brings one closer to the core of life itself, a mystery best understood not by grasping but by feeling. In welcoming elemental energies and the fairies who channel them, we are reminded of the quiet power in yielding to nature's wisdom, in finding balance within ourselves and the world around us. In these moments of alignment, the presence of fairies serves as a gentle yet profound assurance that we are not alone, that there are ancient allies among us who have long safeguarded the beauty, balance, and mystery of life itself.

Chapter 3
Spiritual Connection

Beyond the whisper of leaves, the murmur of streams, and the warmth of fire, there lies a realm accessible only to those willing to look inward and cultivate a quiet, receptive heart. Building a spiritual connection with fairies requires an inner journey, a kind of exploration where each step draws one closer to the mysteries of both the external world and the depths of the self. To connect with these ethereal beings, one must move beyond perception alone, stepping into a realm of intention, respect, and attunement that can only be reached through a genuine alignment of spirit.

Fairies are perceptive beings, attuned to the energies that permeate their surroundings, including the emotions and intentions of those who seek their company. Thus, preparation for connecting with fairies begins not in ritual but in stillness and presence. By nurturing a spirit of openness and reverence, one becomes a vessel ready to receive the subtle communications that fairies offer. This process requires a quieting of the mind, allowing one to listen not with the ears but with the spirit, to feel beyond the body and into the energy of each moment.

Meditation serves as a vital tool in building this connection. Through meditation, one learns to quiet the noise of everyday thoughts, creating a stillness where fairy energies can be sensed. A simple yet effective practice is to sit in a natural space—a forest, a meadow, near a body of water—where fairies are likely to dwell. Closing one's eyes and focusing on the breath, one begins to shift from the outer world to an inner space, letting go of mental chatter and allowing the mind to settle. With each inhale, one draws in the surrounding energy, and with each exhale, one releases any tension or expectation, becoming a vessel of openness. In this state, fairies may feel the invitation, sensing the individual's sincere intention to connect, to learn, and to respect their presence.

This openness is essential, for fairies respond to a purity of spirit rather than external words or actions. Just as we feel drawn to people who emit kindness and sincerity, fairies gravitate toward those whose hearts are open and respectful, whose intentions are free from selfish desire. In this realm of spiritual connection, one finds that the language of fairies is a silent one, spoken through feeling, sensation, and intuition. Fairies may respond to a meditative presence with subtle signs—a gentle breeze that stirs at an unexpected moment, a feeling of warmth, or even an inexplicable sense of companionship that lingers in the air.

Introspection is another valuable aspect of building a spiritual connection with fairies. By turning inward and reflecting on one's own energy, thoughts, and emotions, one learns to approach fairies with a clear and receptive spirit. Fairies often mirror the energies they encounter; they respond not to demands or expectations but to a humble openness that aligns with nature's own rhythm. Before seeking to connect with fairies, it is wise to look within, releasing any negative emotions or thoughts that might disturb the delicate balance of energy. Setting an intention—whether it is gratitude, learning, or simply experiencing presence—anchors the connection, creating a spiritual foundation upon which fairies may feel comfortable approaching.

For those who seek to further strengthen this bond, spending time in nature with mindful awareness deepens the connection with both the environment and the fairies who dwell there. Walking through a forest, feeling the earth underfoot, observing the intricate patterns of leaves, and noticing the play of light and shadow, each of these small acts brings one closer to the rhythm of nature. This mindful presence signals to fairies a respect for their world, inviting them to reveal themselves in subtle ways. With time, one may begin to feel a heightened awareness of the unseen energies, as though the forest, the water, or the sky itself were alive and observing. It is within these quiet moments that the presence of fairies can be felt most acutely.

Harmonizing with fairy energy also involves cultivating an inner balance that resonates with the natural world. Just as nature follows cycles of growth, decay, and renewal, fairies are sensitive to energies that are calm, grounded, and aligned with this rhythm. Practices such as grounding exercises, breathwork, and visualizations of earth's stability help one to resonate with these frequencies. A simple grounding technique involves sitting on the earth, visualizing roots extending from the body into the soil, connecting with the pulse of the earth below. This grounding not only helps to center the spirit but also fosters a resonance with the energy of earth fairies, whose very essence is bound to the earth's stability and nurturing power.

Breathwork, too, is a bridge that connects the human spirit with fairy energy. Deep, mindful breathing brings one's awareness fully into the present moment, calming both body and mind. Each breath taken with intention becomes a pathway to connect with the unseen, to attune oneself to the subtle energies that surround. The act of breathing becomes a conversation of sorts, an exchange between the individual and the energies of the natural world, signaling one's presence and openness to the fairies who may be near.

Fairies, however, reveal themselves in their own time. Patience is essential, for the connection cannot be rushed or forced. Just as one must wait for a bud to bloom, so too must one allow the connection with fairies to unfold organically. They may appear as a fleeting sense of energy, a lightness that comes and goes, or even a gentle whisper that stirs the heart with a feeling of kinship and trust. In these moments, one senses that a bridge has been crossed, that the unseen realm of fairies has opened to reveal its presence, responding to the invitation of a quiet, open spirit.

When fairies choose to respond, they may offer signs—symbols that carry meaning only to the one who perceives them. A feather, a small stone that catches the eye, or the scent of flowers carried on the breeze may all be ways in which fairies signal their acknowledgment. These signs are subtle, meant to inspire reflection rather than offer direct answers. They remind the seeker that the path to understanding is not linear, that the true nature of connection with fairies lies in experiencing the mystery and honoring it without the need for control or explanation.

In these moments of connection, one may also feel a shift within, as though a part of oneself has awakened to a truth that was always there but often overlooked. Fairies, in their gentle way, guide us to rediscover our own spirit, to embrace the quiet spaces within, and to recognize that we, too, are part of nature's great design. By connecting with them, we step into a circle of life, a shared space of energy and reverence that transcends the boundaries between human and elemental, between the physical and the spiritual.

As this bond deepens, the relationship with fairies becomes a journey of inner transformation, where each encounter is a mirror, reflecting both the beauty and the mystery of the natural world. The connection shifts from a simple act of seeking to a profound dance of energies, a friendship between beings whose worlds are intertwined. With each moment of presence, with each quiet act of respect, the veil between the worlds grows thinner, revealing the sacred in the everyday, a reminder that magic is not separate from life but woven into its very fabric.

Thus, in this gentle communion with fairies, the seeker finds not only the presence of these beings but a path to self-discovery, a journey where the boundaries between nature and spirit dissolve, and one becomes fully immersed in the eternal rhythm of life.

As the bridge to the fairy realm grows stronger, so too does one's ability to sense and understand the subtle ways in which fairies communicate. Their language is not one of spoken words but of energy, emotion, and signs, woven into the rhythm of nature. Building a spiritual connection with fairies invites one to engage with deeper techniques of visualization, sensory attunement, and receptivity to the hidden messages within the environment. For those who seek a closer relationship with these beings, the journey is one of heightened awareness and a profound trust in the unseen.

Visualization offers a potent way to bridge the gap between realms. By learning to see beyond physical reality and open the mind's eye, one can begin to perceive the presence of fairies in all their luminous subtlety. A practice to initiate this involves sitting in a quiet, natural space and closing one's eyes, then allowing the mind to envision the elemental energies surrounding that space. Envision the gentle glow of earth energy rising from the ground, the cool flow of water energy in nearby streams, the flickering warmth of fire within sunlight or flame, and the light, swirling currents of air moving through leaves and branches. As the visualization deepens, one may begin to sense the fairies associated with these elements, their forms appearing as soft, shifting lights or as shadows just at the edge of perception.

This practice of visualization is not about forcing an image but rather allowing it to reveal itself naturally. In the presence of fairies, the imagination becomes a bridge, not one of illusion but of invitation—a space where the unseen can make itself known. This visual journey can awaken an intuitive sight that makes it easier to perceive fairies even when one's eyes are open, as the natural world itself begins to reveal its hidden inhabitants. A rustling leaf, a glimmer of light, or an inexplicable movement may hint at a fairy's presence, gently suggesting that one's visualization has invited them closer.

Attuning to the environment also enhances this connection. Each element—the earth beneath, the water flowing, the fire burning, and the air surrounding—carries the energy and presence of fairies. A heightened sensitivity to these elements opens the doorway to experiencing their guardianship firsthand. One way to attune is by paying close attention to changes in the environment; a sudden stillness, an unusual sound, or even a shift in temperature can all be signs that a fairy is near. By observing and accepting these shifts without questioning or analyzing them, one aligns with the rhythm of nature, allowing fairies to communicate through the subtleties of the physical world.

Fairies often communicate through signs, symbols, and sensations, their messages hidden within the fabric of daily life.

These signs vary based on the element with which the fairy is aligned. Earth fairies might reveal their presence through the unexpected discovery of a beautiful stone, a feather, or a rare flower. Water fairies may manifest as the calming sound of flowing water or the sudden appearance of ripples in still water, while fire fairies may reveal themselves through a warm sensation or a spark of light. Air fairies, with their elusive and delicate nature, may be sensed through the movement of wind or even the soft whisper of leaves. To recognize these signs is to deepen the connection with fairies, interpreting their subtle communications as one would read an ancient language, each symbol carrying a message that only the heart can truly understand.

To deepen one's receptivity to these messages, it is essential to cultivate a state of open awareness—a meditative state where one listens with all the senses, allowing intuition to lead the way. In this state, it becomes possible to hear beyond ordinary sounds, to feel beyond ordinary sensations, and to perceive beyond ordinary sight. The more one practices this state, the clearer the fairy messages become, as the mind releases control and allows the spirit to perceive.

With time, fairies may even offer a response to one's presence through subtle signs of interaction. A brief yet intense feeling of joy, a sudden chill, or a sense of lightness may signal that a fairy is near, observing and acknowledging the connection. At times, these signs may carry specific meanings—a tingling sensation on the skin may be a fairy's way of granting permission to enter a particular space, while a warm glow felt within could indicate a fairy's acceptance of one's intentions. Fairies reveal themselves only to those who are patient, kind, and open-hearted, offering these responses as gestures of trust.

Beyond signs and symbols, fairies often communicate through what some describe as "whisperings of the heart." These are not words, but a form of inner knowing or gentle intuition that arises without prompting. It may be an urge to explore a specific area, a sense of being drawn to a certain tree or stone, or even a feeling of warmth and peace that fills one's entire being. These whisperings are the fairies' way of guiding one along a spiritual path, inviting the individual to explore and experience life in a state of constant wonder and openness. Through this form of communication, fairies encourage a shift in perspective, from seeing nature as a mere backdrop to recognizing it as a living, breathing entity filled with wisdom and presence.

For those who wish to go further, specific practices can help strengthen this communication. One such practice involves creating a "fairy space" or small altar in nature or at home—a sacred place dedicated to fairies and the elements. This space might contain stones, feathers, candles, or plants, arranged thoughtfully as a gesture of respect and gratitude. Spending time in this space, speaking softly to the fairies or simply sitting in silence, reinforces the intention to connect, creating a bridge that makes it easier for fairies to reveal their presence. Over time, one may notice the energies in this space shift and change, a sign that fairies have accepted the offering and inhabit the space with gratitude.

As the connection deepens, one's life becomes filled with subtle but meaningful encounters with fairies. They appear not to dazzle or entertain, but to share their wisdom, to remind us of nature's cycles, and to awaken a deeper sense of responsibility for the natural world. Each encounter teaches us patience, respect, and a sense of wonder that leads us to view life as a sacred journey, enriched by the companionship of these timeless beings.

In this deepened bond, fairies become more than guardians of nature; they are companions, guides, and teachers, each interaction a step in the dance between worlds. They offer a mirror to our own souls, showing us the beauty of simplicity, the importance of balance, and the transformative power of presence. Through their teachings, we learn to respect the silence of the forest, the wisdom of flowing waters, the warmth of the flame, and the breath of the wind. Each of these elements becomes a passageway to understanding, each fairy a reflection of the mysteries within and around us.

With each encounter, the line between human and fairy, seen and unseen, fades, leaving in its place a shared journey of discovery and connection—a reminder that, though our worlds may be different, they are bound together by the same forces, the same energies, the same dance of life that unites all beings. Through the presence of fairies, we are drawn ever closer to a deeper truth: that within nature's whispers and the quiet spaces of the heart lies a world rich with wisdom and wonder, a world that opens only to those who seek with reverence, humility, and an open spirit.

Chapter 4
Preparation for Rituals

To step into the world of fairy rituals is to honor both the visible and invisible aspects of the natural realm. Each ritual begins not with words or actions but with an intentional preparation that creates harmony between the self and the energies of fairies. Before inviting these beings into any practice, it is essential to purify both body and spirit, creating a state of openness and readiness for the subtle work ahead. This preparation is as sacred as the ritual itself, setting the foundation upon which the energies of the fairies can connect, communicate, and collaborate.

To begin, one must undertake a process of energetic and mental cleansing. Fairies, being finely attuned to energy, respond most readily to environments and individuals that reflect purity and clarity. A practical method to cleanse the energy is by using herbs known to purify and align with fairy realms, such as lavender, sage, and rosemary. Lighting a small bundle of dried sage or a lavender sprig, one can move through the ritual space, allowing the smoke to clear away any stagnant energy, creating an environment where fairies feel welcomed and respected. While doing this, focus on releasing any stress or distractions, envisioning the space filling with a soft, welcoming light.

Crystals, too, serve as powerful allies in this preparation phase, resonating with the subtle vibrations that attract fairies. Amethyst, clear quartz, and rose quartz carry gentle energies that fairies recognize, each stone possessing a different quality that harmonizes with the ritual. Amethyst, for instance, opens intuition and establishes spiritual clarity, while clear quartz amplifies the energy of intention, and rose quartz nurtures an atmosphere of love and kindness. By placing these stones in the ritual space or carrying one as a personal talisman, one aligns with the energies that fairies are drawn to, signaling both respect and openness.

As important as the environment is, so too is the state of mind and spirit. A brief meditation or moment of introspection before beginning ensures that any lingering thoughts, worries, or doubts are set aside. A helpful practice here is to focus on the breath, visualizing each inhale as a gentle flow of light entering the body, and each exhale as a release of any negative or unnecessary energy. As one's mind settles, there arises a sense of clarity and peace, creating a mental and emotional state that mirrors the purity of the ritual space. This internal harmony signals readiness to the fairies, allowing them to feel welcomed by a spirit that is calm and grounded.

The use of natural items further prepares the space and oneself for the presence of fairies. Flowers, leaves, or small branches from trees carry the essence of nature within them, inviting fairies to join in the ritual. The selection of these items should be intentional, each piece chosen with care and respect, acknowledging that every flower, leaf, and stone is part of a greater whole. Wildflowers such as daisies, lilies, and forget-me-nots are particularly connected to fairies, while branches of oak, elder, and willow have long been sacred to these beings. Arranging these items thoughtfully in the ritual space, or wearing a flower crown or a garland, enhances the sense of harmony and creates an atmosphere that feels both natural and sacred.

Once the space and self are prepared, an invocation of the elements—earth, water, fire, and air—further establishes the ritual foundation. Calling upon the energies of each element invites fairies associated with them, while also creating a balanced space that aligns with the natural world. To invoke earth, one may place a stone or crystal on the ground, touching it briefly to feel its grounding energy. For water, a small bowl of fresh water may be set nearby, symbolizing the flow of emotions and intuition. A candle can serve as the representation of fire, adding warmth and a soft glow to the space, while a feather or an incense stick honors air, filling the space with gentle movement or fragrant smoke. This simple act of honoring the elements invites fairies to join, bridging the physical and energetic realms in preparation for the ritual.

As these preparations conclude, one final act solidifies the alignment: setting an intention. Fairies resonate with purpose and clarity; they respond to intentions that are sincere and attuned to the values of nature, kindness, and balance. Speaking aloud or quietly within, one can state the purpose of the ritual—a simple sentence or phrase that encapsulates the heart of the practice. Whether it is for healing, gratitude, protection, or guidance, stating the intention completes the preparations, signaling both to oneself and to the fairies the readiness to move forward.

The effect of this preparation extends beyond the ritual, weaving a subtle connection between the seeker and the fairy realm. Fairies recognize the respect and care taken in creating this environment, and they respond by lending their energy, aligning themselves with the intention and purpose of the practice. The ritual space becomes a bridge, a point of meeting where human and fairy can coexist, interact, and work in harmony.

Through these acts of preparation, one finds that the ritual's success lies not in grand gestures but in the quiet, intentional details. Each step, each element chosen and arranged, is a gesture of reverence, an acknowledgment that the path to fairy connection is one of patience, respect, and attunement to nature's gentle rhythm. The foundation is thus laid for a practice that is as much a journey inward as it is an invitation outward, creating a space where fairies feel honored and inspired to share their wisdom.

As the seeker delves deeper into ritual preparation, the act becomes not only a way to honor the fairies but also a powerful means of aligning one's own energy with the essence of the natural world. Fairies are sensitive beings, and they respond most readily to spaces that vibrate with intentional care and respect. Thus, each act of preparation serves as both an offering to these beings and an invitation for their presence. In this part of the journey, we move from creating a welcoming environment into refining that space, consecrating objects, and establishing a dedicated altar where fairies may feel truly at home.

The altar, whether set up in a natural outdoor space or in a quiet corner indoors, is a central point of focus and connection. A carefully chosen cloth or natural surface, such as wood or stone, can serve as the base, grounding the altar in the element of earth. Each item placed upon the altar carries its own energy, creating a miniature universe that mirrors the harmony of nature. Small bowls filled with earth, water, or salt honor the elemental fairies, while flowers, leaves, crystals, and candles offer symbolic beauty that fairies can recognize and appreciate.

The act of consecrating the altar and its objects infuses the space with purpose. Consecration is more than a ritual—it is a vow of respect, a statement of intention that transforms ordinary items into vessels of spiritual energy. To consecrate, one can lightly touch each item on the altar, imbuing it with an intention specific to its role. For example, a crystal might be consecrated to amplify energy, a candle to embody illumination, and a flower to represent nature's inherent beauty and wisdom. Each touch is a silent promise to honor the presence of fairies, to treat each element as a sacred connection to the unseen world.

Programming these objects deepens the alignment, allowing each piece to hold a specific energy or purpose that supports the ritual's goals. Crystals, in particular, respond well to programming, their structure naturally holding energy and intention. By holding a crystal and setting a specific intention—such as clarity, protection, or compassion—one can imbue it with a purpose that resonates with the ritual's aims. This charged crystal then becomes a focal point on the altar, a beacon that both attracts and stabilizes fairy energy, forming a bridge between realms. Likewise, other objects can be programmed for harmony, protection, or gratitude, each one carefully chosen to reflect an aspect of the desired connection with fairies.

To maintain an altar that remains energetically vibrant, regular attention is essential. Just as nature thrives with gentle care, so too does an altar benefit from mindful tending. Cleaning and rearranging the space periodically renews its energy, ensuring that it does not become stagnant. Sprinkling water or placing fresh flowers on the altar refreshes it, while lighting a candle or incense invites warmth and movement. These acts are simple but meaningful, each one signaling to fairies that this is a dedicated, living space where their presence is honored and valued.

Once the altar is prepared, selecting the ideal moment for the ritual becomes the final piece of preparation. The timing of a ritual holds significance, as natural cycles and celestial patterns affect the energies present. Aligning a ritual with the phases of the moon or particular times of day enhances the connection, lending additional power to the practice. For example, rituals performed at dawn or dusk align with the fairies' own rhythms, as they are often most active during these transitional times. Similarly, certain moon phases resonate with different types of fairy energy: the full moon for abundance, the new moon for new beginnings, and the waning moon for release.

Beyond the physical preparation, entering a state of presence and grounding anchors the practitioner firmly within the space. A simple grounding practice, such as visualizing roots extending from one's feet into the earth, helps create a steady foundation. In this state, the mind becomes calm, the spirit open, and the energy harmonious, ready to receive and interact with the fairy realm. The fairies, sensing this intentional alignment, are drawn not only to the physical preparations but also to the mindful energy of the practitioner. In this way, the entire preparation becomes a sacred offering, a doorway that welcomes fairies to join the ritual in unity and trust.

By aligning the ritual with both intention and nature's own rhythms, the practitioner steps into a dance with the fairies, one where each movement and each gesture reverberates with a purpose. The altar, carefully arranged and consecrated, becomes a portal, an energetic space where human and fairy can meet. Each object upon it carries the intention set forth, each symbol a point of connection to the unseen. As the practitioner stands before this altar, grounded and aligned with the natural rhythms, the boundary between worlds softens, creating a space where communication with fairies flows seamlessly.

In these moments, the preparations reveal their deeper meaning—they are not merely acts performed to impress or appease, but profound gestures of respect and harmony. The fairies, perceiving the sincerity in these preparations, respond not only with presence but with a shared purpose, entering the space as allies, guides, and teachers. The entire ritual, born from this preparation, becomes a dance of energies, a moment where the boundaries between human and fairy dissolve in shared respect for the sacredness of nature.

As one's connection with fairies deepens through this dedicated preparation, the relationship shifts into a true partnership. The ritual space, charged with intentional energy and aligned with nature's cycles, becomes a place of shared creation, where fairies and humans work together. And through this collaboration, the practitioner begins to see ritual not as a mere act but as a living practice, one that reflects the harmonious flow of life itself—a reminder that, in honoring fairies, we also honor the interconnectedness of all beings.

Chapter 5
Fairy Invocation

To call upon fairies is to enter a realm of intentional communication, a delicate and profound act that invites these elemental beings to join in ritual. Unlike human interactions, invoking fairies requires an intuitive approach, one where words carry not just meanings but vibrations aligned with respect and clarity. Fairies respond to purity of intention and to those who approach them with humility, honoring their ancient presence as guardians of nature's mystery. This invocation is not a demand; it is a gentle request, a respectful call that opens a channel between realms, inviting fairies to share their wisdom and energy.

Before speaking the words of invocation, it is essential to quiet the mind and set a clear intention. Fairies are perceptive, sensitive to the underlying emotions and energies woven into the ritual. They respond to those who come not out of curiosity alone, but from a genuine desire to connect, to learn, and to work in harmony with the forces of nature. Thus, preparing oneself with mindfulness ensures that the invocation resonates deeply, becoming a beacon that fairies can sense and trust.

A chosen phrase or set of words for invocation should be simple yet intentional, crafted to honor the fairies while expressing the purpose of the ritual. Phrases such as, "Guardians of the natural world, spirits of earth, water, fire, and air, I invite your presence in peace and harmony," serve as an open, humble call. These words do not command; they gently open a door, signaling to fairies that their presence is invited and appreciated. One might also personalize the invocation based on the element associated with the fairies being called, acknowledging their unique qualities and roles. An invocation to earth fairies, for example, might reference their strength and grounding nature, while a call to water fairies could invite their soothing, flowing presence.

While words carry weight, the energy behind them is equally essential. Speaking from the heart and allowing each word to carry sincerity imbues the invocation with a frequency that fairies are drawn to. As one speaks, it is helpful to focus not only on the words themselves but on the feelings they evoke—feelings of gratitude, respect, and wonder. These emotions, when woven into the invocation, create a vibration that fairies recognize as genuine, inviting them to respond in kind.

Once the invocation is spoken, silence follows, creating space for the fairies' presence to reveal itself. This pause is a vital part of the invocation, as it signals openness to receiving rather than controlling the outcome. In this silence, the mind remains still, the heart receptive, attuning to any subtle shifts in energy that may indicate a response. A sudden warmth, a sense of lightness, or an unexpected sound could be signs that the fairies have drawn near, acknowledging the invitation with their presence. Patience here is essential; fairies respond not to urgency but to calm, centered awareness, and they often make themselves known in delicate, fleeting ways.

In addition to the spoken invocation, small gestures can reinforce the sincerity of the call. Lighting a candle, offering a flower, or placing a few drops of water upon the ground adds a physical component to the invitation, grounding the intention in action. Fairies recognize these gestures as tokens of respect, appreciating the time and care taken to create a harmonious environment for connection. A candle flame, symbolizing the warmth and vitality of the fairy realm, becomes a focal point for the invocation, a small yet potent representation of the energy shared between human and fairy.

As the invocation takes shape, grounding oneself within the ritual space enhances the stability of the connection. Visualizing roots extending from the body into the earth creates a steady base, grounding the practitioner's energy and anchoring the invocation within nature itself. This grounding practice not only centers the self but also reflects the stability that fairies associate with those who work respectfully with nature. By aligning one's energy with the earth, the invocation resonates more deeply, amplifying the call and creating a secure, harmonious space that welcomes the fairies' presence.

Throughout the invocation, it is essential to maintain a spirit of humility. Invoking fairies is not an act of control; it is a cooperative call, an invitation that recognizes fairies as ancient and wise beings. This mindset transforms the invocation from a mere request into a sacred act of alignment, a recognition that fairies, as guardians of nature, choose to respond only to those who approach them with reverence. Holding this respect in one's heart strengthens the bond, as fairies are naturally drawn to individuals who honor their role within the greater cycle of life.

As one completes the invocation, a feeling of gratitude serves as the final, silent word. Gratitude acknowledges both the possibility of connection and the presence of the fairies, even if they choose not to appear in tangible ways. Expressing thanks at the end of the invocation, either aloud or inwardly, signifies that the practitioner values the fairies' wisdom and energy, regardless of the form their response takes. This gratitude forms a gentle closure, an honoring of the fairies' autonomy and an appreciation for their potential guidance.

The invocation, though simple, is profound. It is a quiet act of faith, a reaching out across the boundary between realms with open hands and an open heart. The fairies, perceiving the purity of this call, may respond with their energy, offering a subtle presence that enriches the ritual. In this way, the invocation serves as a bridge, connecting human and fairy in a shared moment of trust, unity, and respect.

Thus, the words of invocation become more than mere sound; they transform into a language of the spirit, a heartfelt call that transcends spoken words. The fairies, sensing this sincerity, may draw near, forming a partnership that breathes life into the ritual and infuses it with a sacred energy that can only arise when both human and fairy join in harmony. Through this act, one realizes that the invocation is not simply a ritual—it is a shared dance of intention and presence, an invitation to enter into the timeless world of fairies.

Once the door to the fairy realm has been respectfully opened, the invocation deepens. Each fairy type holds its own resonance, responding to different words, tones, and rhythms that call them forth from their respective elements. To cultivate a harmonious, lasting connection, practitioners may turn to specific chants, mantras, or gentle melodies that are finely attuned to the frequencies of each fairy type. These sacred sounds go beyond mere words, touching the essence of the element itself, awakening a presence that lies just beyond sight.

When invoking earth fairies, the tone of the chant is slow, steady, and rhythmic, mirroring the grounding energy they embody. Simple words, spoken with intention and repetition, create a vibration that echoes through the body and into the earth, forming a pathway for earth fairies to approach. A soft, low chant such as "Rooted in earth, strong and wise, guardians of stone and soil, I honor your presence" carries an energy that resonates deeply. The words are secondary to the sensation they inspire; it is the steady pulse of the voice, like the beat of a drum or the rustle of leaves, that draws earth fairies into the space, inviting them to join the ritual with their steady, grounding presence.

For water fairies, who respond to fluidity and grace, the invocation takes on a melodic, almost whispering quality, as though it were carried on a gentle stream. Water fairies are drawn to softness, a gentle tone that mirrors the flow of water. Chanting in a slow, wave-like rhythm creates a calming energy that invites them to emerge. Words like "Flow of life, pure and true, fairies of rivers, lakes, and seas, I call upon your essence" might be spoken in a way that feels like the ebb and flow of a river, allowing the rhythm to move naturally. Water fairies respond to the invitation with subtle signs—perhaps a cool breeze, a faint trickle of water nearby, or an unmistakable feeling of fluidity surrounding the space.

The invocation for fire fairies carries a livelier, more energetic tone. Fire fairies are responsive to passion, intensity, and warmth, and they resonate with a clear, focused chant that ignites the ritual with a vibrant energy. A mantra such as "Flicker of flame, spark of light, fairies of fire, I honor your might" is spoken with confidence and focus, each word carrying a hint of power. Fire fairies respond to this intensity, often revealing their presence through a sudden increase in warmth, the flicker of a candle flame, or a sense of excitement and movement within the space. Through this fiery invocation, one calls upon the fairies of transformation, inviting them to bring their light and vitality to the ritual.

For air fairies, the invocation must be light, swift, and free-flowing, reflecting their ethereal nature. A chant to invite them may be more of a whisper than a spoken word, a breath that captures the freedom of the open sky. "Wind and breeze, pure and free, fairies of air, come dance with me" invites these fairies with a sense of playfulness and openness. Air fairies are drawn to a sense of ease and fluidity, responding to a tone that feels as light as the wind itself. Their presence may be felt as a sudden gentle breeze, a sense of expansiveness, or even a soft, fleeting sound that stirs the air.

Each invocation, while unique to the element, shares an underlying quality of respect and openness. The words and tones chosen are crafted not to demand, but to welcome, acknowledging the fairies as allies and friends rather than servants. By choosing words that honor their qualities, one cultivates a spirit of partnership, a shared moment where human and fairy energies align. This mutual respect is key to successful invocation; fairies are sensitive to intention and respond to those who approach them with a genuine sense of reverence.

Once the invocation has been voiced, maintaining a focused state of mind is essential for deepening the connection. Fairies are naturally drawn to those who are present in the moment, centered within themselves and open to the subtle energies around them. To enhance this focus, one might practice visualization, imagining the presence of the fairies as glowing forms around the ritual space, each embodying the essence of their element. Visualizing the warmth of fire, the coolness of water, the groundedness of earth, and the lightness of air, one begins to feel a shift in the atmosphere, a quiet assurance that the fairies are near.

In moments of strong attunement, one may find that the fairies respond in ways that feel almost conversational. The flicker of a candle, a rustling of leaves, or a subtle shift in air may be their way of acknowledging the invocation. Paying close attention to these signs reinforces the connection, as fairies often communicate through sensations and symbols rather than words. A spark in the candle may suggest their presence, while a sudden breeze could indicate their approval. These signs, though subtle, deepen the relationship, creating a silent dialogue where both fairy and human energies are shared.

As the invocation draws to a natural close, it is essential to offer gratitude, both in spirit and word. Fairies resonate with those who honor their presence, and a simple expression of thanks, spoken or silent, serves as a powerful acknowledgment of the connection formed. A phrase like "Thank you, spirits of earth, water, fire, and air, for your presence and guidance" completes the invocation, allowing the energies to settle. This gratitude forms a respectful closure, signaling to the fairies that their presence is appreciated, whether they choose to remain or return to their realm.

Through these invocations, one learns that the essence of connection with fairies lies in balance and respect. Each chant, each word, is a note in a song that bridges worlds, resonating with a timeless rhythm that fairies instinctively recognize. The invocation becomes an art, a mindful practice where every sound, every intention, aligns with the elements, creating a channel through which fairies and humans can communicate. This connection, once established, serves as the foundation for the journey ahead, each invocation a step further into the mysterious, harmonious world of fairies.

Chapter 6
Healing Ritual

Within the ethereal presence of fairies lies a potent gift—a healing energy that, when carefully channeled, can restore balance to both body and spirit. Fairies, attuned as they are to the cycles and rhythms of nature, embody the wisdom of renewal and transformation. To perform a healing ritual with their assistance is to invite these gentle forces to flow into spaces of imbalance, releasing tension, soothing emotions, and fostering harmony within. Yet, as with all fairy work, healing through fairies requires careful preparation, openness, and a spirit attuned to nature's cycles.

The first step in a fairy healing ritual is establishing a space that welcomes this work. As fairies respond to environments of harmony and purity, the ritual space must reflect these qualities. One might begin by cleansing the area with herbs like sage, cedar, or lavender, creating an atmosphere that invites fairies' energy to enter freely. Water also plays a role in this preparation, as a bowl of fresh water placed in the ritual space serves as a mirror, reflecting an intention for clarity and purity. These elements align the space with the fairy realm, forming a sanctuary where their healing energy can flow without obstruction.

To channel fairy healing, the practitioner must also prepare internally, centering the mind and calming the heart. This can be achieved through a simple grounding exercise. Visualizing roots extending from one's feet deep into the earth, one draws upon the earth's stability and grounding force. As one breathes, they feel the earth's energy rise through their body, anchoring the spirit within the present moment. This grounded state is essential, as fairies' healing energies respond best to a practitioner who is fully present, free from the pull of scattered thoughts or distractions.

With the space and self prepared, the next phase is inviting the specific energies of fairies associated with healing. Earth fairies, with their nurturing essence, are often called upon for physical healing, as their connection to soil, plants, and stones aligns with the body's own need for strength and resilience. Water fairies, whose energy flows with intuition and emotion, are ideal for emotional healing, soothing deep feelings and releasing old wounds. Inviting these fairies into the ritual is done with a gentle invocation, spoken with gratitude and clarity. Words such as, "Fairies of earth and water, I invite your healing presence to join me, to bring peace, strength, and renewal" offer a respectful call, setting the intention for their aid.

The practitioner, having created a grounded, welcoming space, then begins the ritual by attuning to their own energy. Placing hands over the heart or on areas of the body where healing is desired, one invites the fairies to channel their restorative power. Focusing on the sensation of warmth or a gentle tingling, one opens to the possibility of the fairies' presence, feeling their energy as a soft glow, a comforting weight, or a sense of relief and calm. Visualizing this energy as a green or blue light, one envisions it flowing through the body, dissolving tension, releasing pain, and restoring balance. This visualization strengthens the bond with the fairies, as their healing energy is drawn into alignment with the body's natural rhythms.

In working with fairy healing energy, the role of plants and herbs takes on particular significance. Herbs such as chamomile, peppermint, and rose petals are known for their calming and rejuvenating properties, and their use in the ritual amplifies the connection to earth fairies. The practitioner may place these herbs around the ritual space, burn them as incense, or brew a tea to drink before the ritual begins. Each herb, chosen with intention, carries a unique frequency that fairies recognize, deepening the resonance between fairy and human. Fairies of earth and water, sensing the presence of these plants, draw nearer, lending their healing energy in harmony with nature's own medicine.

As the ritual unfolds, the practitioner may also incorporate touch, gentle movement, or breathwork to guide the healing energy throughout the body. Each breath becomes a channel, drawing in the fairies' essence and circulating it to areas in need. A technique known as "fairy breath" involves inhaling slowly, imagining the breath as a wave of light that spreads warmth and ease with each exhale. This breathwork not only enhances the healing energy but also reinforces a sense of unity with the fairies, whose presence is often felt through shifts in air, temperature, or subtle sounds.

Throughout the ritual, it is essential to maintain a sense of openness and trust in the fairies' guidance. Healing with fairies is an intuitive process, one that unfolds naturally without force. Fairies may lead the practitioner to move their hands to different areas, to pause in stillness, or to close their eyes and simply listen. By trusting these impulses, one allows the fairies to guide the flow of energy, shaping the ritual to match their wisdom and insight.

Closing the ritual involves a gesture of gratitude, acknowledging both the fairies and the healing energy that has been shared. This gratitude can be expressed with a simple phrase, "Thank you, fairies of earth and water, for your presence and your healing." One might also leave a small offering—flower petals, a stone, or a few drops of water—returning a token of appreciation to nature. This act of gratitude completes the cycle of energy, affirming that healing is a shared gift, one that honors both giver and receiver.

In the gentle silence that follows, the practitioner may find that the energy of the fairies lingers, a quiet assurance of their continued presence. This experience of fairy healing serves as a reminder of nature's resilience, of the body's ability to heal in harmony with the natural world. Through this ritual, the practitioner has not only received the fairies' aid but has deepened a connection that continues to nurture and support long after the ritual itself has ended.

Thus, the healing ritual becomes a sacred exchange, a partnership between human and fairy, where energy, intention, and respect create a space for profound transformation. Each step, from preparation to gratitude, reflects an understanding that healing flows best when it aligns with the cycles and spirits of nature. In this shared journey, both fairy and human energies blend, revealing that true healing is a balance of body, spirit, and the unseen forces that support us in every moment.

As the initial steps of the healing ritual unfold, the energies deepen, weaving together the presence of the fairies with the intentions of the practitioner. The energy within the space becomes alive, receptive, and ready to support the body and spirit through deeper channels of renewal. Here, the ritual expands from its initial stages into a profound act of communion with fairies, where visualization and breathing techniques guide the energy and open a path to profound healing.

At this stage, visualization becomes an active bridge, focusing the mind and spirit on the fairy energy now present. The practitioner may begin by imagining a gentle, luminous light enveloping them—a light that resonates with the color of the elements being channeled for healing. Earth fairies may manifest as a warm green or earthy brown glow, symbolizing grounded stability and strength, while water fairies bring shades of blue or silver, representing emotional balance and fluidity. This light forms a cocoon, an energetic sphere that holds and protects, surrounding the practitioner with the supportive, healing presence of the fairies.

As this visualization strengthens, the practitioner may feel subtle shifts in sensation—an inner warmth, a tingling, or a deep sense of calm. These are indications that the fairy energy is beginning to interact with the body's own energetic system, aligning and attuning to areas of tension, fatigue, or imbalance. In this state, the practitioner opens fully, allowing the healing energy to move where it is most needed, whether to a specific part of the body, an emotional block, or a general feeling of stress. Each sensation is received without resistance, as the fairies, sensitive to the energy of acceptance, channel their healing more readily when one's spirit is open and receptive.

Breathwork further enhances this connection, acting as a rhythm that guides and stabilizes the energy within. Each inhale draws in the fairies' essence, filling the practitioner with a renewed sense of vitality, while each exhale releases what is no longer needed, creating space for healing to take root. A technique known as "elemental breath" can deepen this practice. In elemental breath, the practitioner visualizes inhaling through the colors associated with the fairies' elements—breathing in green for earth, blue for water, red for fire, or white for air—and feeling the corresponding energy enter and flow through their body. With each breath, the fairy energy aligns more closely, supporting the body's natural cycles of balance and release.

As this breathing continues, the practitioner might experience flashes of insight or feelings rising to the surface. In fairy healing, emotional energy often emerges in subtle ways, as fairies encourage a gentle release of old memories, emotions, or patterns that no longer serve one's well-being. In these moments, the energy may feel both comforting and revealing, as though guided by a wise presence that knows precisely where healing is most needed. Fairies, ever attuned to the soul's subtleties, guide this process, inviting the practitioner to recognize and gently let go of these old energies.

To anchor this energy, the practitioner may engage in gentle movements, touching areas of the body that feel tense or blocked, acknowledging them with compassion. By placing hands over the heart or upon the abdomen, for example, the practitioner creates an additional point of focus, signaling to the fairies where healing is intended. This physical contact, combined with the fairies' energy, enhances the ritual's effect, forming a tactile reminder that healing encompasses both the physical and energetic bodies.

As the healing energies deepen, signs of response from the fairies may become apparent. One might sense a sudden stillness, as if the air itself were holding its breath, or a faint shift in light as though the fairies themselves were acknowledging the alignment achieved. These are subtle messages, signs that the fairies recognize the connection and that their healing presence flows in synchrony with the practitioner's energy. While fairies rarely communicate in direct forms, these delicate shifts signify their approval and engagement, a confirmation that the ritual is in balance with the natural world.

Closing the ritual with respect and gratitude is as essential as the invocation itself. As the healing process reaches a natural conclusion, the practitioner may visualize the fairy energy gently releasing, offering thanks for the presence and aid of these beings. A soft phrase, such as "Thank you, fairies of healing and balance, for your gift and guidance," serves as both acknowledgment and farewell. To honor their support, a small offering can be placed upon the altar or left outdoors—a few flowers, a crystal, or a sprinkle of fresh herbs—as a gesture of reciprocity.

One final visualization brings the ritual to a close, sealing the healing energy within. The practitioner may imagine the light surrounding them slowly merging into their own aura, becoming part of their personal energy field, carrying the fairy energy forward even as the fairies themselves withdraw. This visualization solidifies the healing received, encouraging it to integrate within the body and spirit, enhancing the lasting effects of the ritual. The space gradually returns to a quiet, peaceful state, filled with a sense of completion and renewal.

In the days following, one may notice subtle shifts in well-being—a renewed sense of calm, physical ease, or even an emotional lightness that emerges gradually. This is the fairy energy continuing its work, a gentle reminder that healing is not confined to a single moment but is an ongoing journey. Fairies, with their connection to nature's cycles, understand that healing occurs in phases, unfolding quietly, just as seeds sprout and grow over time. This extended effect serves as a testament to the bond formed in the ritual, a continuous blessing that fairies leave behind, supporting the practitioner long after the ritual has ended.

Through this ritual, one experiences not only the fairies' healing touch but also a profound reminder of nature's inherent wisdom and kindness. The healing ritual becomes more than a moment of relief; it transforms into a living relationship with fairies, a path where both practitioner and fairy share in the sacred cycle of growth, release, and renewal. In this communion, the boundaries between human and fairy, healer and healed, begin to dissolve, leaving a deep, enduring harmony that resonates in both spirit and nature.

Chapter 7
Protection Ritual

To invite the fairies into the role of protector is to call upon energies that guard, nurture, and maintain the sacred balance within one's space and spirit. Fairies, ever sensitive to the needs of the natural world, bring their own wisdom and energy to the creation of protective barriers that safeguard against disruptive forces. By calling upon their guidance, the practitioner aligns not only with the fairies' strength but also with the subtle energies of nature that reinforce boundaries in both seen and unseen realms. The protection ritual with fairies serves as a shield, a way of creating harmony by inviting their watchful presence to ward off negativity.

The initial steps of a protection ritual begin, as always, with intentional preparation of both the practitioner and the environment. The space should be carefully cleansed and centered, free of distractions or lingering energies that might affect the clarity of the ritual. Herbs with protective qualities—such as rosemary, sage, or basil—are excellent allies in this phase, and their smoke or scent purifies the air, creating an environment that invites only positive, balanced energies. Fairies are drawn to spaces that resonate with clarity, and this cleansing ensures that the energies in the ritual space are harmonious, grounding the area as a sanctuary.

The choice of symbolic items for protection is an essential component of the ritual. Crystals, symbols, and specific plants act as both physical reminders of the fairies' presence and channels through which their protective energy can flow. Black tourmaline, for instance, has long been valued for its grounding and protective properties, making it a favored crystal in fairy protection rituals.

By placing it near doors or windows or holding it in hand during the ritual, one establishes a boundary that both strengthens the physical space and calls upon the fairies to support this barrier. Similarly, ivy, with its enduring and resilient nature, can be woven into a protective charm or placed in the space, representing the fairy's protective embrace.

Once the space is ready, the practitioner enters into a state of quiet focus, grounding themselves with deep breaths, connecting to the earth below and the sky above. This grounding centers the spirit and clears the mind, creating a stable foundation upon which the protection ritual will unfold. Visualizing roots from the feet reaching deep into the earth allows one to connect with the fairies of earth, whose stabilizing energies lend strength and endurance to the ritual. As the breath flows in, one draws in this grounding energy, feeling its weight and presence throughout the body, anchoring them firmly within the moment.

Next, the practitioner speaks a simple invocation, welcoming the fairies of protection to join in this sacred task. Words such as, "Fairies of strength and guardianship, I invite your presence, to watch over this space, to create a barrier of harmony and safety," create an atmosphere of respect and alignment. This invocation is not a demand; it is a respectful call that signals the practitioner's openness to fairy guidance and partnership. The fairies, sensing this genuine intent, respond in subtle ways, their energy woven into the air, grounding the space in protection.

The focus then shifts to creating an energy barrier, a shield formed by visualization and the fairies' energy. The practitioner may begin by imagining a soft yet resilient light—a gentle glow that emerges from within and expands outward, forming a sphere of protection around the space. This light, infused with the essence of earth fairies, feels strong yet gentle, like the roots of a tree reaching deeply into the soil. Envisioning this light expanding, it takes on the form of an energetic shield, encompassing the entire area, a veil through which only harmonious energies may pass. This visualization serves as a channel, a means by which fairies lend their strength to fortify the boundary, wrapping the space in their protective presence.

To deepen this barrier, symbols of protection are then activated within the space. Placing symbols, such as a small stone circle or a charm made from twine, along with natural objects that carry the fairies' energy, builds a physical counterpart to the energetic shield. These symbols are placed with care around the perimeter of the ritual area or in specific points like entryways or windows, and each one is consecrated with a soft touch or whispered intention. The practitioner might say, "With this stone, I honor your strength. May it stand as a guard, a symbol of protection." Each item placed strengthens the energetic structure, each touch enhancing the fairies' involvement and recognizing their role in the ritual.

An integral aspect of the protection ritual is the establishment of a mental boundary. This internal act mirrors the external protections and creates a balance between the outer and inner worlds. By envisioning a calm, resilient mind, one reinforces the idea that protection begins within. This inner boundary signifies one's own role in the ritual—recognizing that while fairies provide guidance and strength, the practitioner's focused intent completes the protective shield. A simple affirmation, such as "I am grounded, I am safe, I am surrounded by the fairies' protection," acts as a seal, creating a mental framework that enhances the strength of the ritual's energy.

To conclude, a gesture of gratitude closes the ritual. Thanking the fairies for their presence and protection acknowledges their role and respects their choice to assist. Words of gratitude, such as "Thank you, guardians of this space, for your strength and guidance," honor the relationship formed, reminding the practitioner that protection is not only received but shared. A small offering, such as placing a flower, a handful of herbs, or a few drops of water near the entrance to the space, signifies this gratitude. The fairies recognize and appreciate such offerings, as these simple gestures of respect reaffirm the practitioner's commitment to harmony.

As the ritual concludes, a feeling of calm assurance may fill the space. The protective energies, supported by the fairies, will continue to linger, creating a sense of stability and resilience. This ritual serves not only to protect the physical environment but also to strengthen the bond between fairy and human, uniting both in the shared commitment to maintaining a balanced, safe space. The protective barrier, both physical and energetic, endures as a reminder that one's own spirit is a sacred space, safeguarded by the fairies and grounded in nature's timeless strength.

With the protective energies established in the initial ritual, the focus now turns to reinforcing, deepening, and maintaining this barrier over time. The connection between the practitioner and the fairies grows stronger with each gesture of respect, each focused intention. Fairies are beings who move naturally through cycles and rhythms, and they guide those who seek protection to do the same, teaching that true protection is not static but a dynamic, evolving energy. By learning techniques to strengthen, seal, and renew the protective boundary, the practitioner creates a lasting, harmonious shield that endures through life's shifting energies.

To seal the protective barrier, concentration and grounding are essential. Fairies respond most powerfully to those who approach them with centered intention, and thus, focusing fully on the protective space is the first step. The practitioner begins by placing their hands on the earth or a chosen grounding object, allowing any scattered thoughts or distractions to fall away. Closing the eyes, one visualizes roots extending deep into the ground, anchoring the self and absorbing strength from the earth below. This grounding anchors the practitioner's energy within the space, reinforcing stability and creating a connection that the fairies naturally align with.

As the energy deepens, the practitioner can use a technique known as "circle sealing" to encapsulate the protection. This involves moving clockwise around the perimeter of the space, either physically or mentally, tracing an invisible line that completes a circle of strength. While moving, the practitioner may chant a phrase that holds protective power, such as, "Circle of light, strong and bright, protect this space day and night." This phrase, spoken rhythmically, creates a frequency that resonates with the fairies, sealing the boundary with intention and reverence. This circular movement represents a cycle, symbolizing an unbroken connection with the fairy realm, who lend their strength to guard the space.

Grounding this barrier with specific objects further solidifies the protective energies. Small stones or crystals, chosen for their alignment with protection, can be placed at each cardinal point—north, south, east, and west. Each stone is consecrated with a touch or spoken word, like, "In this direction, I call upon protection," and represents a pillar of strength. North, often linked to earth, symbolizes stability; south, aligned with fire, represents courage; east, the direction of air, brings clarity; and west, associated with water, offers emotional peace. The fairies, attuned to these elemental directions, sense this alignment and lend their energy to reinforce the shield.

To renew and maintain the barrier, periodic attention is essential, as fairies respond well to rituals that respect natural cycles. A weekly or monthly practice, adapted to the practitioner's needs, strengthens the fairies' connection with the space and reinforces their presence. This can be as simple as lighting a candle and offering words of gratitude, or placing a fresh flower on the altar to symbolize harmony and protection. Fairies are naturally drawn to these small acts, recognizing the practitioner's intention to honor the space continuously. These gestures renew the protective boundary, ensuring it remains vibrant and active.

In addition to physical objects, visualization and breath play a central role in maintaining protection. The practitioner may take time each day to sit quietly within the space, breathing slowly and visualizing the protective light surrounding them. Imagining this light as a strong, shimmering veil, the practitioner envisions it pulsing gently with each breath, renewing its strength. Breathing in, they draw energy from the fairies into the protective sphere; breathing out, they release any disturbances or negative energy that may have gathered within. This practice not only reinforces the barrier but also keeps the practitioner's own energy balanced and resilient, harmonized with the fairies' presence.

Over time, the practitioner may develop an intuitive sense for shifts in energy, sensing when the boundary requires reinforcement or renewal. Fairies, ever sensitive to energies, often communicate subtle cues when adjustments are needed—perhaps through a flickering candle, an unexpected cool breeze, or a feeling of restlessness within the space. Paying attention to these signals allows the practitioner to adjust the ritual according to the fairies' guidance, maintaining the strength of the protection in harmony with natural energies. This intuitive partnership with the fairies is a living, evolving practice, shaped by both the practitioner's awareness and the fairies' wisdom.

Detecting the approach of negative or disruptive energies is a skill that the fairies can help cultivate. With their guidance, the practitioner learns to recognize slight shifts in the atmosphere, sensations that hint at imbalances or intrusions within the space. For example, a sudden heaviness, a sense of unease, or a lack of airflow may indicate the need for immediate attention. In such moments, fairies encourage grounding practices to clear the energy, such as the use of salt at entry points or sprinkling lavender water around the space. These actions neutralize disturbances, reinforcing the boundary while also respecting the cycles of renewal that fairies hold dear.

Fairies also guide practitioners in the use of grounding rituals to dispel lingering unwanted energies. One such method involves standing within the space and visualizing a waterfall of light descending from above, washing over the body and the room. This light clears away any residual energy, carrying it into the earth where it is transformed and purified. As this visualization unfolds, one might say, "With this light, all that does not serve shall be cleansed and renewed." Fairies, drawn to such gestures, lend their energy to the cleansing, ensuring that the space remains clear and harmonious, a sanctuary of peace and protection.

The ritual closes with an expression of gratitude, signaling respect and appreciation for the fairies' ongoing protection. A phrase such as "Thank you, fairies of protection, for your strength and guidance," acknowledges their presence and reinforces the bond between realms. A small offering—a sprinkle of water, a handful of wildflowers, or a feather—can be left at the edge of the space or placed within the altar as a final act of appreciation. The fairies receive these gestures with warmth, recognizing the respect that underlies the protective partnership.

In the quiet that follows, a profound sense of peace often fills the space. The protective barrier, now strong and resilient, stands as a testament to the cooperation between human and fairy, a shared commitment to maintain balance and guard against harm. Through this ritual, the practitioner not only secures their physical environment but strengthens their own inner resilience, learning from the fairies how to cultivate peace in the face of change.

This extended protection ritual becomes a journey in harmony with nature, where fairies serve as both guardians and guides, showing that true protection is a balance of awareness, respect, and reciprocity. Each act, from the lighting of a candle to the placement of a stone, honors the ancient energies that weave through all things, forming a sanctuary of enduring safety and calm.

Chapter 8
Prosperity Ritual

Inviting fairies into a prosperity ritual is an act of welcoming abundance, not merely as material wealth but as a holistic flow of opportunity, well-being, and harmony. Fairies, guardians of nature's cycles, understand abundance as something that arises naturally when balance is honored and intentions align with the good of all. To attract prosperity with their guidance is to step into nature's rhythm of growth and fulfillment, allowing opportunities to unfold with trust and respect. The prosperity ritual, therefore, becomes a harmonious request to receive, share, and nurture abundance with a heart aligned to fairy wisdom.

To begin, the ritual space is carefully prepared to reflect the qualities associated with prosperity: openness, light, and the symbols of natural abundance. Objects associated with growth—flowers, herbs, and crystals—become potent allies, creating an atmosphere that both fairies and the practitioner can feel. Golden or yellow flowers, such as marigolds or sunflowers, bring a sense of warmth and radiant energy to the ritual, symbolizing the sun's nourishing influence on all life. Sprigs of basil, mint, or cinnamon, known for their association with prosperity, may be placed on the altar or in small bowls around the space, their scents mingling to invite positive, abundant energy.

Crystals amplify this energy, each with its own resonance that aligns with prosperity. Citrine, often regarded as a stone of abundance, radiates with a vibrant energy that fairies recognize as a symbol of growth and joy. Aventurine, another favored crystal, holds the essence of opportunity, guiding intentions with clarity and confidence. These stones, placed thoughtfully in the ritual space, serve as focal points for the fairies' energy, inviting them to bless the ritual with the same natural cycles of flourishing they uphold in the world around them.

To further enhance the space, a single green or gold candle may be lit, representing the intention for prosperity. As the candle flame flickers, the practitioner envisions it as a beacon, calling forth the fairies associated with abundance. This flame, infused with the practitioner's energy, acts as a symbol of light, growth, and the life force that sustains prosperity. With each breath, the flame grows in significance, becoming a central element of the ritual that both fairies and the practitioner focus upon, as its warmth and glow symbolize the prosperity that will flow into life.

Once the space is prepared, the practitioner grounds themselves through a simple breath exercise, inhaling deeply and exhaling any tension or limitation that may cloud the intention. Fairies are naturally sensitive to clarity of spirit, and this grounding process ensures that the practitioner's energy resonates with sincerity and openness. With each breath, one feels a greater connection to the earth beneath and the natural cycles that support life and growth. This alignment creates a fertile ground upon which intentions can be planted, much like seeds in a garden, ready to flourish with care and attention.

The invocation is then spoken, a respectful call that invites fairies to bring their guidance and blessing to the ritual. A simple phrase, such as "Fairies of abundance and growth, I invite your presence with gratitude and trust," signals the practitioner's willingness to enter into this partnership. Fairies respond to such calls when they are filled with respect and humility, understanding that the practitioner's intention is to create prosperity not only for themselves but for the greater good. This invocation shifts the ritual into an active state, a shared moment where the fairies' presence begins to permeate the space, lending their energy to nurture the seeds of abundance.

With the fairies' presence invited, the practitioner sets their intention for prosperity. This intention is most potent when it arises from a place of gratitude and clarity, recognizing that prosperity encompasses far more than material gain. Speaking the intention aloud, the practitioner might say, "May abundance flow into my life as freely as sunlight upon leaves, nourishing all that I undertake and allowing me to share freely." The intention, spoken with conviction, becomes a powerful declaration, aligning with the fairies' own understanding of abundance as a cycle that benefits all who honor it.

A visualization technique called the "Prosperity Bloom" then guides the practitioner further. Sitting quietly, they imagine themselves as a plant rooted deeply in the earth, nourished by its strength and stability. With each inhale, they envision drawing in light and warmth from the fairies, like sunlight that causes the plant to grow and flourish. This energy flows up from the earth and through the roots, reaching the heart and extending outward like branches, symbolizing the spread of opportunities, joy, and abundance. With each breath, the light grows brighter, filling the space and radiating outward, carrying the intention for prosperity into the universe.

To channel the fairies' energy more directly, the practitioner may also hold a crystal, such as citrine or aventurine, in their hand while visualizing. The crystal becomes an anchor, a vessel that holds the energy of prosperity and can be revisited even after the ritual ends. By focusing on the crystal's warmth and weight, one connects to the fairies' guidance and trusts in the unfolding process of growth, much like a seed transforming into a flowering plant. This crystal can be kept on the altar or carried as a reminder of the fairies' blessing and the commitment to nurture prosperity mindfully.

In addition to visualization, a spoken affirmation reinforces the intention. Phrases like "I am open to receive abundance in all forms," or "Prosperity flows to me and through me, enriching my life and the lives of others" carry the energy of conviction and openness. Fairies, attuned to intention and resonance, sense the clarity in these words and strengthen the practitioner's connection to the natural cycle of giving and receiving. This affirmation solidifies the practitioner's role within the ritual, marking a promise to work in harmony with the fairy energies and the prosperity they inspire.

Closing the ritual with gratitude acknowledges the fairies' presence and their assistance in opening the path to abundance. A soft phrase, "Thank you, fairies of growth and prosperity, for your presence and your blessing," honors their guidance and affirms the intention with respect. A small offering—perhaps a flower, a sprinkle of seeds, or a few drops of water—is left as a token of gratitude, returning to nature a part of what has been requested. This offering serves as a reciprocal act, a way to honor the fairies' role in supporting abundance, much like the act of returning nourishment to the soil from which a plant grows.

In the quiet that follows, the energy of the ritual continues to flow, a subtle yet potent reminder that prosperity, like all natural cycles, unfolds with patience and care. The fairies, having sensed the respect and gratitude of the practitioner, lend their continued support, fostering an atmosphere of abundance that transcends the ritual itself. The ritual space remains vibrant, filled with a quiet assurance that prosperity will manifest, nurtured by the fairies' wisdom and the practitioner's trust in the flow of life.

Through this prosperity ritual, the practitioner experiences a partnership with fairies that reflects nature's rhythms—a dance of giving and receiving, of growth and generosity. The fairies, ever watchful and wise, guide the seeker into alignment with these rhythms, teaching that true prosperity is both received and shared, rooted in gratitude and balanced by mindful intent. In their presence, the path to abundance becomes clear, shaped by respect for the cycles of nature and the magic that fairies bring to life's most essential journeys.

As the energies of prosperity settle into the ritual space, the practitioner and the fairies embark on a deeper journey—one that transforms the intention into tangible manifestations. Prosperity, in its true sense, aligns not only with receiving but with cultivating a mindset of gratitude, trust, and balance. Fairies, being guardians of nature's endless cycles, lend their wisdom to guide the practitioner in creating a continuous flow of abundance that enriches life on multiple levels. Through advanced techniques of manifestation, visualization, and signs of fairy presence, this ritual becomes a dance of harmonizing intentions with nature's rhythms.

To begin, the practitioner revisits their initial intention, refining it through visualization to set the energy in motion. This visualization goes beyond a simple image; it becomes a sensory experience that infuses the ritual with life. The practitioner may close their eyes, envisioning a garden brimming with vibrant blooms, fruits, and sunlight—a symbol of abundance and prosperity. Each flower represents an aspect of prosperity—health, relationships, creativity, or opportunities—that the practitioner wishes to nurture. In this garden of intentions, fairies move as guardians and caretakers, tending to each bloom, guiding the energy as it roots and flourishes. The visualization weaves together the practitioner's desire for prosperity with the fairies' role as keepers of growth and transformation.

With each breath, the practitioner deepens their connection to the fairies and their garden of abundance. This breathing technique is called "Prosperity Breath." On each inhale, the practitioner draws in the feeling of vitality and fulfillment, envisioning the fairies enhancing each aspect of prosperity. On each exhale, they release any doubts, fears, or limitations that might hinder the flow of abundance. As this breathing continues, a feeling of warmth and lightness fills the body, signifying the alignment between the practitioner's intention and the fairies' energy. The fairies sense this alignment and respond, weaving their energy into the visualized garden, nurturing the intentions with the same care they give to the natural world.

Next, to anchor the energy and bring the intentions into tangible form, the practitioner employs a ritual known as "Manifestation Stones." A selection of small stones or crystals—such as aventurine, citrine, and green jade—is arranged around the ritual space, each one symbolizing an aspect of prosperity. The practitioner holds each stone, speaking a phrase of affirmation specific to that intention, such as "This stone represents abundant creativity," or "With this stone, I invite financial stability." By setting these affirmations, each stone becomes a focal point, a physical representation of prosperity. These stones are charged with both fairy energy and the practitioner's focused intent, becoming symbols that can be revisited long after the ritual is complete.

The fairies, drawn to these objects of intention, lend their presence to the stones, imbuing them with the vibrational energy of abundance. The stones, now charged, act as conduits between realms, each one a tangible reminder of the fairy partnership in the journey toward prosperity. Placing the stones on an altar or carrying them in daily life serves as a touchstone, a way to keep the intentions alive and supported by the fairies' quiet guidance.

In addition to stones, symbols of gratitude are introduced to strengthen the ritual. As fairies resonate deeply with appreciation, expressions of gratitude amplify the flow of prosperity. The practitioner may place a small bowl of grains or seeds—symbolic of nourishment and growth—on the altar as a sign of thankfulness for what they have already received. This offering becomes an acknowledgment that prosperity, both given and received, is a continuous cycle. The fairies sense this gratitude, understanding that the practitioner honors the balance of taking and giving. This act of gratitude, woven into the ritual, ensures that the energy of abundance remains sustainable, supported by a spirit of generosity.

Signs of response from the fairies may now become apparent, subtle hints that the intentions are aligned with nature's flow. One might notice a sudden sparkle of light, a faint warmth, or a soft breeze moving through the space—signs that fairies are guiding the energy of the ritual. Fairies communicate in whispers and gestures, often leaving behind symbols in nature to signify their approval. After the ritual, the practitioner may notice small feathers, unexpected flowers, or stones catching their attention—fairy signs that affirm the connection established in the ritual, reminding the practitioner that prosperity flows in harmony with nature's gifts.

To ground the ritual and integrate the fairy energy, the practitioner completes a visualization known as the "Abundance Flow." In this technique, they imagine a gentle river flowing through their life, carrying opportunities, joy, and fulfillment. This river of abundance moves freely, nourished by the fairies and the natural world, filling every corner of the practitioner's life. With each breath, the practitioner becomes one with this flow, trusting that prosperity will arrive in many forms, each one a gift from the unseen world. This visualization solidifies the belief that prosperity is an open, living energy, guided by the fairies and shaped by the practitioner's own intentions.

The final act of the ritual is to release the fairies with deep gratitude, acknowledging their wisdom and assistance in manifesting prosperity. A soft phrase, such as "Thank you, fairies of abundance, for your guidance and generosity," sends the fairies off with respect, honoring their role in the ritual. The practitioner might leave an offering of honey, flowers, or a few grains by a tree or in the garden as a last gesture of gratitude, returning to nature a portion of what has been received. The fairies, sensitive to such gestures, recognize the sincerity of the offering, and their presence lingers in the subtle warmth of the ritual space.

In the days and weeks that follow, the practitioner may observe the ways in which prosperity begins to manifest, sometimes in unexpected or subtle forms. An opportunity might arise, a creative idea may blossom, or a moment of kindness may create a ripple of positivity. These are signs that the fairy energy continues to support the practitioner's intentions, reminding them that prosperity flows as a natural cycle, best received with trust and nurtured with gratitude. This ongoing connection with the fairies teaches that abundance is not a single event but an evolving relationship, a partnership that deepens as one remains open to both giving and receiving.

Through this ritual, prosperity becomes a state of being, a connection to the fairies that transcends material wealth and encompasses a life of balance, fulfillment, and gratitude. The fairies, wise in the ways of nature's cycles, guide the practitioner toward a prosperity that is sustainable, rooted in respect for the earth and all its gifts. This partnership reveals the deeper truth of abundance, that it is woven from intention, trust, and a shared journey with the unseen forces that nurture all things into growth.

Chapter 9
Alignment with Nature

To connect with fairies is to immerse oneself in the rhythms and cycles of nature, as these beings are the essence of the natural world itself. They exist within each season, echo in the rise and fall of the sun, and move with the flow of rivers and the growth of trees. Thus, aligning oneself with nature is not merely an act of observation; it is an invitation to live in harmony with the earth and all of its creatures. In doing so, the practitioner opens a doorway to a more profound connection with fairies, embracing a shared journey where respect and reciprocity guide each step.

The first step in alignment is to cultivate presence in nature, allowing each walk, each moment outdoors, to become a ritual of connection. Fairies respond to those who tread lightly, who walk with awareness, treating every leaf, stone, and drop of water as sacred. As one moves through a forest or along a river, the practitioner consciously quiets the mind, letting go of distractions and instead focusing on each sound, scent, and texture. Listening to the wind through the trees, feeling the earth underfoot, and observing the subtle signs of life all serve to attune the practitioner to nature's rhythm. This mindful presence draws the fairies near, as they recognize a heart open to the language of the natural world.

Nature observation practices are central to this alignment, inviting the practitioner to notice patterns, cycles, and subtle changes within the landscape. By observing the behavior of plants, animals, and the shifting elements, the practitioner begins to understand how fairies live within these rhythms. The changing colors of leaves, the budding of flowers, and the cycles of the moon all carry messages, offering insight into the fairies' world. Fairies are often present at the edges of these transitions, appearing at dawn and dusk, during the quiet hours between day and night, or at the first bloom of spring. By tuning into these moments, the practitioner becomes aware of the subtle shifts that mark the fairies' presence and influence.

Outdoor meditations deepen this connection, serving as a bridge between the physical and fairy realms. A simple practice is to sit quietly beside a tree, closing the eyes, and breathing in harmony with the sounds of nature. Visualizing roots extending from one's body into the earth, connecting with the roots of the tree, brings a grounding energy that fairies recognize as a gesture of respect and unity. Each inhale draws in the stability of the earth, while each exhale releases any lingering tension or distraction, creating a calm, balanced state that aligns with the fairies' gentle energy. In this grounded awareness, one may sense a soft shift—a brush of cool air, a faint rustling, or even an inner feeling of warmth, all subtle signs of fairy presence.

Another practice, known as "Listening to the Land," invites the practitioner to stand or sit in a natural space and focus on the sounds that emerge. This exercise is not merely about hearing but about tuning into the layers of sound: the movement of the wind, the call of birds, the hum of insects, each note forming a symphony that fairies inhabit. By surrendering fully to these sounds, the practitioner cultivates a sensitivity that resonates with the fairies' presence. The fairies respond to this focused listening, often leaving subtle signs—a feather, a glimmer of light, or a gentle shift in the breeze—as acknowledgments of the practitioner's openness to connection.

To further align with nature, the practitioner observes the cycles of the seasons, each one holding unique energies that mirror the fairies' own transitions. Spring, a time of renewal, vibrates with the energy of new beginnings, inviting fairies associated with growth and vitality to emerge. Summer, full of warmth and abundance, resonates with fairies of light and joy. Autumn, with its falling leaves and cooling air, marks a time of release and transformation, drawing fairies connected to change and reflection. Winter, a time of stillness, invites fairies who work quietly, encouraging introspection and the conservation of energy. Embracing these seasonal energies aligns the practitioner with the fairies' natural rhythms, fostering a relationship that grows and shifts with each cycle.

In addition to observing nature, creating simple offerings strengthens the bond with fairies. An offering is an act of gratitude, a small gesture that acknowledges the fairies' guardianship over the earth. Placing flowers, leaves, or a few grains of food upon a stone or at the base of a tree sends a silent message of respect. These offerings, chosen mindfully, resonate with the fairies' energy, inviting them to draw closer. In return, fairies may leave subtle gifts—a fallen feather, a unique stone, or an unexpected feeling of peace—signs of their appreciation and presence.

Engaging in rituals that honor natural events also aligns the practitioner with the fairies. Observing the solstices, equinoxes, and phases of the moon places one in harmony with cycles that the fairies themselves honor. For example, during a full moon, fairies of intuition and inner light are especially present, offering guidance to those who seek connection. Creating a small ritual—lighting a candle, offering water, or singing softly beneath the moonlight—invites the fairies' blessing and affirms a shared reverence for nature's rhythms.

Throughout this journey of alignment, patience is essential. Fairies reveal themselves only gradually, drawn to those who show respect through actions rather than expectations. Alignment with nature is a commitment, a practice that grows over time, marked by moments of connection that become richer and more profound with each interaction. This process teaches that alignment with nature and the fairies is less about seeking and more about simply being present, open, and willing to learn from the world around us.

As the practitioner continues these practices, they may notice a shift in perception, an ability to sense energies previously overlooked. Each day spent in alignment with nature brings a deeper understanding of the fairies' quiet wisdom and their role as guardians of balance. This alignment reveals that prosperity, protection, and peace flow naturally when one lives in harmony with the cycles that fairies cherish and protect.

Thus, the journey of aligning with nature becomes a path of transformation. The practitioner discovers that in each leaf, breeze, and season lies a lesson, a whisper of fairy magic that speaks of balance, resilience, and interconnectedness. The fairies, guardians of this wisdom, guide the practitioner into a life where every moment becomes a celebration of nature's beauty and an invitation to live with gratitude, humility, and harmony.

As the journey of alignment deepens, the practitioner is called to move beyond observation, embracing practices that intertwine their life with nature's rhythms in profound ways. Fairies, ever attuned to the cycles of the earth, draw closer to those who honor the changing patterns of the moon, the sun, and the seasons. Each cycle, each transition within nature, becomes an opportunity for the practitioner to synchronize their energy with the fairies' world, fostering a bond that transcends the physical and connects deeply with the timeless flow of life.

One of the most powerful practices for deepening alignment with fairies is working with the lunar cycles. The moon's phases mirror nature's rhythm of growth, release, and renewal, resonating with the fairies' own cycles. During the new moon, a time of beginnings and intentions, earth fairies are particularly present, nurturing seeds of growth and supporting new undertakings. The practitioner, sitting quietly under the dark sky, sets intentions by speaking them softly or writing them on a piece of paper. Placing this intention near a living plant or burying it in soil sends a message to the fairies of earth, who recognize this act as an invitation to aid in nurturing these desires from seed to bloom.

As the moon waxes, growing brighter, the practitioner shifts their focus toward actions that bring intentions to fruition. Water fairies, sensitive to the flow and movement of energies, align with this phase, supporting creativity, intuition, and emotional depth. This phase is an ideal time for outdoor rituals near water—a river, lake, or even a small bowl of water placed under the moonlight. The practitioner may gently ripple the water, watching as it catches the moon's light, symbolizing the expansion and manifestation of intentions. Water fairies respond to this fluid energy, lending their guidance as the practitioner's goals begin to take shape.

At the full moon, the energy peaks, a time of culmination and abundance. Fire fairies, embodying light and vitality, are drawn to this phase, which represents the height of energetic power. Standing under the full moon, the practitioner might light a candle or small fire, feeling the warmth as a representation of fulfillment. As the flame dances, one may express gratitude for what has come to fruition, acknowledging the fairies' role in nurturing these outcomes. This practice not only honors the full moon but invites the fairies to celebrate the harvest, the fruition of seeds sown with intention.

As the moon wanes, the energy shifts toward release and reflection, aligning with the quiet, introspective fairies of air. This phase encourages letting go, making space for renewal and preparation for the next cycle. The practitioner might perform a simple ritual of release, such as writing down thoughts or emotions they wish to release, then placing the paper into the wind or a gentle stream, allowing it to be carried away. This act symbolizes surrender, an offering to the air fairies, who guide the practitioner toward clarity and lightness, helping dissolve what no longer serves. The fairies of air recognize this practice as an alignment with the rhythm of nature, a willingness to let go and trust in the cycle's flow.

Alongside the lunar cycle, observing the changing seasons strengthens this alignment with nature's timeless rhythm. Fairies, whose energies shift with each season, reveal different aspects of their world during each phase. In spring, as new life emerges, fairies connected to growth and renewal are especially active, inviting the practitioner to join in celebrating rebirth. Planting seeds, tending to a garden, or simply spending time in a field or forest during spring aligns the practitioner's energy with the fairies of vitality, who sense this devotion to nature's renewal and respond with warmth and support.

Summer is a time of abundance, light, and activity, a season when fairies of joy and vitality move vibrantly through the world. This is a time for rituals of celebration, for dancing, singing, and sharing with others, embodying the exuberant energy that summer fairies bring. Spending time in sunlight, offering fresh flowers, and creating joyful gatherings draw fairies close, as they are drawn to moments of genuine happiness and expression. Each act of joy resonates with summer's energy, inviting the fairies to participate and bless the practitioner's life with vitality and connection.

Autumn, a season of change and preparation, calls for reflection and the fairies of transformation. This time of year invites rituals of gratitude, where the practitioner acknowledges the bounty they have received. Gathering leaves, placing them on an altar, or creating small tokens of thanks for the fairies recognizes the natural cycle of giving and receiving. Fairies of autumn guide the practitioner in releasing what has served its purpose, just as trees shed their leaves, preparing the practitioner to enter a state of rest and reflection, aligning with nature's quiet preparation for winter.

Winter, with its stillness and introspection, aligns with fairies who guard the depths of rest and renewal. This season invites the practitioner to embrace practices of quiet meditation, reflection, and inner work. Sitting beneath bare trees, breathing in the crisp air, and listening to the silent world, one attunes to the energy of winter fairies. These fairies teach the value of rest, of turning inward to cultivate the seeds of new growth that lie dormant within. By embracing this stillness, the practitioner learns to respect the quiet cycles within themselves, honoring the fairies' wisdom that true growth often arises from periods of rest and renewal.

To deepen this seasonal alignment, the practitioner may also keep a nature journal, recording observations, experiences, and reflections with the fairies throughout the cycles. By noting changes in the landscape, the presence of specific flowers, animals, or weather patterns, one builds an understanding of the environment's subtle shifts and the fairies' role within it. This journal becomes a testament to the practitioner's dedication, a living record of alignment with the natural world that reveals patterns, insights, and a growing awareness of the fairies' presence.

Over time, this alignment with lunar and seasonal cycles creates a flow where the practitioner feels in harmony with nature's pulse, their life resonating with the fairies' timeless rhythm. The cycles of growth, abundance, release, and rest become more than concepts; they are lived experiences, a dance of balance, resilience, and renewal. This ongoing journey strengthens the bond with fairies, inviting their guidance in ways that transcend ritual, becoming a constant presence, a quiet support in daily life.

Through this alignment, the practitioner finds that their relationship with fairies moves beyond fleeting interactions and blossoms into a partnership built on trust and shared purpose. Living in alignment with nature's cycles, one realizes that the fairies' wisdom is embedded in each breath, each season, each quiet moment under the sky. This journey of alignment transforms life into a sacred experience, where human and fairy walk side by side, sharing the beauty and depth of the natural world, connected by a common rhythm and a shared commitment to the balance and harmony that sustains all things.

Chapter 10
Advanced Energy Work

The work of channeling energy, with fairies as guides, opens a path to understanding and mastering the natural energies that pulse through all of life. These energies, as fairies perceive them, are the invisible currents of earth, air, fire, and water—the elemental forces that sustain balance within the world. By learning to recognize and channel these energies, the practitioner can build a refined sensitivity that deepens their connection to the fairy realm. Here, the fairies serve not only as companions but as teachers, leading the practitioner into advanced practices that refine their ability to channel and harmonize energy.

To begin this journey, one must first cultivate an awareness of the energies that surround and sustain the body, recognizing that every breath, sensation, and emotion is part of an energetic exchange with the natural world. The fairies, masters of subtle energies, respond to this heightened sensitivity, drawn to those who attune themselves with an open heart and a mindful presence. Through basic energy awareness exercises, the practitioner learns to become a vessel, a conduit for the elemental energies that fairies themselves represent.

One foundational practice is known as "elemental grounding," a technique that roots the practitioner in the present moment by connecting them to the four primary elements. Standing barefoot on the earth, the practitioner envisions themselves as a tree with roots extending deep into the soil, drawing upon the stabilizing energy of earth. This grounding provides strength and focus, a foundation upon which energy work can build. Once anchored, the practitioner then opens to the other elements, visualizing air as a gentle breeze around them, fire as a warm glow within, and water as a soothing flow, each element moving through the body in harmony. This exercise establishes balance, aligning the practitioner with the energies of earth, air, fire, and water, which the fairies recognize and resonate with.

With grounding established, the next step is "energy sensing," an exercise that trains the practitioner to feel the subtle shifts and vibrations of fairy energy within their space. Fairies communicate in quiet currents, and by holding one's hands out and moving them gently through the air, the practitioner learns to detect sensations such as warmth, tingling, or coolness. These shifts are the first signs of fairy presence, energy that manifests in response to the practitioner's open intent. By sensing this energy, one begins to discern the qualities of each element: earth as steady, air as light, fire as vibrant, and water as fluid. Each sensation is a message from the fairies, an invitation to deepen the partnership and explore the transformative nature of these energies.

The practice of "energy drawing" follows, an exercise in which the practitioner consciously invites elemental energy into their being. To draw in earth energy, for instance, one may sit on the ground, placing both hands on the earth and visualizing its deep, grounding force rising through the body. The practitioner might feel a sense of stability or a comforting heaviness, as if roots were intertwining with their own energy. To draw upon air energy, standing with arms open and inhaling deeply invokes the lightness of a breeze, bringing clarity and expansion into the mind. Each element is invited with reverence, as fairies lend their presence to enhance these sensations, helping the practitioner feel and channel the unique energies more vividly.

Once a connection with each element is established, the practitioner can begin to create "energy circles." This advanced technique involves forming a circle of energy within the ritual space, weaving the qualities of each element into a unified field that radiates harmony and protection. Starting with earth, the practitioner visualizes a band of green or brown light encircling the space. Moving clockwise, they then add air, visualized as white or blue light, followed by fire, a band of red or orange, and finally water, in shades of blue or silver. This energy circle serves as a sacred container, a place of concentrated elemental presence where fairies can enter and share their wisdom without interference from outside energies. The fairies sense this respect for their realms and respond, often manifesting in subtle shifts in the environment—a warm gust of air, a soft glow, or the scent of earth or flowers.

As energy work progresses, the practitioner may also create "protection rings" for themselves or their surroundings. Unlike an energy circle, which encompasses a ritual space, a protection ring is a concentrated field of energy drawn from a single element for specific purposes, such as grounding, focus, or shielding. To create an earth-based protection ring, the practitioner visualizes a ring of dense, grounding energy encircling their body, providing stability and resilience. This technique is particularly useful in moments of stress or overwhelm, as it acts as a buffer, harmonizing the body's energy with the grounding essence of earth. Fire, on the other hand, may be called upon for confidence and vitality, creating a ring of warmth and light that empowers the practitioner from within.

The fairies, present and guiding during these exercises, offer subtle affirmations—perhaps through a sudden calmness, a tingling warmth, or an unexpected stillness in the air. These signs signal that the fairies are harmonizing with the practitioner's energy work, providing insight and encouragement as the partnership deepens. Over time, the practitioner develops a refined awareness, becoming adept at discerning fairy presence through these shifts, recognizing them not just as companions but as active participants in the flow of energy.

To close an advanced energy work session, grounding and gratitude bring the energy back into balance, honoring the fairies for their presence. The practitioner might place both hands over their heart, visualizing all gathered energy softly returning to the earth, leaving a calm, centered awareness. Offering a soft word of thanks, such as "Thank you, guardians of the elements, for your guidance and presence," acknowledges the fairies' role in the practice. Fairies respond to this gratitude, recognizing it as a sign of respect, and their lingering presence serves as a reminder of the bond formed through each session.

As the practitioner continues to work with these advanced techniques, they begin to sense the energies of earth, air, fire, and water as familiar companions, flowing within and around them as naturally as breath. The fairies, ever watchful and wise, guide this journey, teaching that energy work is not about control but about balance, harmony, and respect for the elements' inherent qualities. Each session, each practice, deepens the practitioner's understanding of the elemental realms, strengthening the connection to the fairies who protect and embody these energies.

In this partnership, the practitioner becomes both student and steward, learning from the fairies while nurturing and protecting the energies that sustain life itself. The journey of advanced energy work transforms, revealing that true mastery is a balance of humility, openness, and a shared reverence for the unseen forces that shape our world. Through this sacred relationship, the practitioner finds a way to walk with the fairies, not just in ritual but in every moment, each breath a part of the endless dance of energy and life.

As the practitioner deepens their relationship with elemental energies, they are called to refine their mastery, moving beyond basic techniques into complex practices that integrate fairy energy with their own. Advanced energy work with fairies teaches the practitioner to not only recognize and channel elemental energies but to shape and harmonize them within specific spaces and circumstances. In this journey, fairies are no longer distant guides but intimate allies, leading the practitioner into realms of transformation, protection, and expanded awareness.

The practice of creating "energy circuits" is one of the most profound ways to channel and direct fairy energy. This technique involves circulating elemental energy within a space, creating a dynamic flow that enhances the atmosphere and brings harmony to all present. To create an energy circuit, the practitioner begins by inviting the presence of each element, honoring earth, air, fire, and water in their respective directions. Moving clockwise, they imagine the energies flowing in a continuous circle, visualizing earth as a grounding force, air as a light breeze, fire as warmth, and water as a fluid presence. Each element interconnects with the next, creating a circuit where energy moves freely, generating a balanced and vibrant atmosphere.

Fairies, who understand the delicate nature of these energies, lend their guidance to maintain balance within this circuit. As the practitioner channels these energies, they may sense the fairies adjusting the flow, gently guiding the circuit's strength and direction. Signs of fairy involvement—such as a sudden warmth, a faint scent of flowers, or the soft rustling of leaves—signal that the fairies are actively harmonizing the energy, helping to shape it into a cohesive and nurturing presence. The circuit thus becomes a dance, a living flow of energy where the practitioner and fairies work together, co-creating an environment of unity and calm.

Building on the energy circuit, the practitioner may also create "elemental channels," a technique that directs each element into specific areas of life or environment based on need. To focus earth energy, for instance, they may concentrate on creating a sense of grounding and stability in the home. This energy, channeled with the fairies' guidance, settles like a reassuring weight, enhancing feelings of security and balance. Air, directed into a workspace, brings clarity and inspiration, its light, expansive quality encouraging new ideas and perspectives. Fire, channeled into social gatherings, generates warmth and connection, while water, directed into spaces of rest, brings calm and healing.

To refine these elemental channels, the practitioner might visualize each element as a distinct color and sensation, breathing into that energy to strengthen the intention. Fairies sense this focus and respond, lending their unique energies to enhance the specific qualities of each element. By holding crystals, symbols, or objects associated with each element while setting these intentions, the practitioner invites the fairies' energy into physical form, anchoring the elemental qualities within the space. These objects become conduits, holding the intention even after the ritual concludes, continuing to shape the atmosphere in alignment with fairy wisdom.

The creation of "energy spheres" represents an even deeper layer of advanced energy work. Unlike circuits or channels, which involve an ongoing flow, an energy sphere is a concentrated field that the practitioner shapes into a self-contained presence. To create an energy sphere, one begins by grounding deeply, connecting to the earth's core. Visualizing a specific elemental energy, the practitioner then draws this energy into their hands, imagining it forming a radiant sphere between their palms. This sphere can embody any element—earth for stability, fire for empowerment, water for healing, or air for clarity—and is used as a tool to project that energy into spaces, objects, or even individuals in need of support.

The fairies, sensing the practitioner's focused intent, guide the process, often enhancing the sphere's strength and purity. For instance, a sphere of water energy may feel especially soothing and cool, a gentle indication that water fairies are amplifying the sphere's healing properties. Once the sphere is charged, the practitioner can release it into the space or direct it toward a specific purpose, trusting in the fairies' continued guidance to channel the energy appropriately. These spheres are potent, carrying the fairies' essence long after they are created, acting as a sustained source of elemental energy that supports the intended purpose.

In advanced energy work, creating "protection rings" for individuals or spaces becomes a practice of both intention and refinement. Unlike basic protective barriers, these rings are woven with the fairies' energy, forming a dynamic shield that adapts to changing energies. To create a protection ring, the practitioner begins by invoking the element most aligned with their intention—earth for grounding, fire for courage, air for mental clarity, or water for emotional stability. Envisioning this element forming a protective circle around themselves or another person, the practitioner calls upon fairies to infuse the ring with their specific qualities, enhancing its resilience and adaptability.

Fairies respond to this request by lending their own protective energy, which may be felt as a subtle shift in temperature, an added sense of strength, or a comforting calmness. This protection ring is not rigid; it flows with the wearer, adjusting as needed to maintain balance. This fluidity is key, as fairies understand that protection is an evolving presence, one that guards without restriction, allowing growth and movement within safe boundaries. The practitioner may renew these rings periodically, refreshing the energy through a simple breath exercise, visualizing each breath as a reinforcement of the protective qualities gifted by the fairies.

To enhance these advanced techniques, practicing "fairy attunement" becomes essential. This involves sitting quietly in a natural space, such as a forest or by a stream, and tuning in to the fairies' presence. By placing a hand on the earth or in water and breathing slowly, the practitioner begins to feel subtle sensations—light tingling, warmth, or an uplifting energy that signals the fairies' response. This attunement helps the practitioner synchronize their energy with the fairies, creating a state of awareness that enhances their capacity to channel and shape energy.

During fairy attunement, the practitioner may receive insights—feelings or images that convey the fairies' guidance on how to refine their energy work. These messages are not always direct; they may come as a sense of calm, a feeling of encouragement, or a spontaneous idea. By trusting these impressions, the practitioner aligns their practice more closely with fairy wisdom, allowing the fairies' presence to shape each technique with natural harmony and insight. This attunement strengthens the connection, creating a bond of mutual respect and collaboration that deepens with each session.

The closing of advanced energy work sessions is an act of gratitude and grounding, a moment to honor the fairies for their guidance and to reintegrate the energies into one's personal space. The practitioner might place their hands over their heart, offering thanks in silent reverence or softly spoken words. A phrase such as "Thank you, fairies of nature, for your wisdom and support" acknowledges their guidance, respecting their role in each technique. Leaving a small token—such as a stone, leaf, or flower—on the altar or in nature symbolizes this gratitude, a gesture the fairies recognize as a continued commitment to alignment with the natural world.

As the practitioner integrates these advanced techniques, they begin to understand that energy work is both a skill and a relationship. The fairies, ever-present and wise, guide not as mere companions but as true partners, shaping each practice into an expression of balance, awareness, and respect. This journey transforms the practitioner's view of energy, revealing it as a shared language that connects the human and fairy realms. Through this work, the practitioner learns that energy flows best when it aligns with the cycles of nature, the wisdom of fairies, and the intention to bring harmony to oneself and the world around them.

In time, this partnership with fairies and their energies evolves into a way of living, where each action, thought, and feeling is part of a larger, harmonious flow. The practitioner, now attuned to the fairies' presence, walks a path of balance and respect, embodying the knowledge that energy is not merely something to wield but a sacred connection to be honored and shared. Through this union, the practitioner and the fairies create a living bond that continues to deepen, a shared journey that celebrates the beauty, resilience, and magic inherent in all things.

Chapter 11
Sharing Wisdom

As the practitioner's journey with fairies deepens, there comes a natural desire to share this sacred knowledge, extending the presence of fairies beyond the personal to those around them. Sharing wisdom is both an act of humility and respect, recognizing that each insight, each connection formed with fairies, is a gift from the natural world meant to be honored and treated with reverence. When wisdom is shared thoughtfully, with sensitivity to the unique path of each seeker, the knowledge of fairies becomes a bridge, opening others to the possibility of connecting with these guardians of nature.

To share fairy wisdom authentically, it begins with the intention to teach with integrity and openness. Fairies respond to those who share with sincerity, valuing the respect for boundaries and the deepening of each individual's unique connection. Thus, the practitioner's role is not to dictate or impose but to guide, creating a space where others can explore and experience fairies in their own way. Teaching fairy wisdom is less about imparting information and more about fostering an atmosphere where curiosity and intuition are encouraged, allowing seekers to form their personal bond with fairies.

Creating a dedicated space for sharing is one of the first steps in guiding others on this path. Whether held in nature, in a quiet indoor space, or through the creation of a small circle, the environment must feel harmonious and balanced, a reflection of the fairies' own presence. Nature is often the most effective setting, as the gentle presence of trees, earth, and open sky invites participants to connect naturally with the energies around them. An altar, simple yet intentional, may be set with symbols of the elements—stones, leaves, water, and candles—to honor the fairies and invoke their presence. This altar becomes a focal point, a reminder that the space is sacred, dedicated to fairies and their teachings.

To initiate a session, grounding exercises bring participants into a state of calm and presence. This practice connects them to the earth beneath, the air around, and creates a shared energy of openness. Simple breathing exercises, where one visualizes roots growing from the feet into the ground, establish a sense of unity, preparing each person to approach the fairies with clarity and respect. The practitioner may invite participants to close their eyes and listen to nature's sounds, to feel the breeze, the warmth of the sun, or the scent of the earth. This moment of grounding, guided by the practitioner's gentle voice, brings everyone into harmony with nature's rhythm, signaling to the fairies that this gathering is held with reverence.

Once the group is centered, the practitioner introduces fundamental concepts of fairy wisdom with simplicity and respect, presenting fairies as elemental beings deeply intertwined with nature. Each person is encouraged to perceive fairies not as distant entities but as presences that can be sensed in the movement of water, the whisper of wind, and the quiet of earth. Rather than speaking of fairies as external beings, the practitioner guides the group to understand fairies as part of the world's living energy. This approach resonates with the fairies' own nature, as they reveal themselves more openly to those who view them as partners rather than mysterious outsiders.

Participants are then invited into practices of awareness, designed to attune them to fairy energy. One of the most accessible methods is a "nature attunement walk," where each person moves slowly and mindfully, observing the landscape with a heightened sense of openness. The practitioner encourages participants to notice small details—the patterns on a leaf, the way light filters through branches, or the rhythm of a flowing stream. Fairies are often present in these subtle aspects, and by attuning themselves to these details, participants enter a state of awareness that invites fairy presence.

As each person begins to connect, the practitioner may gently introduce the concept of "fairy signs"—the ways fairies leave subtle reminders of their presence, often in natural forms like feathers, unusual stones, or delicate patterns in sand or soil. Participants are encouraged to keep an open mind, interpreting signs based on their own intuition and experiences. These signs are messages, gifts that fairies leave as gestures of welcome or guidance, and by noticing them, one honors the fairies' quiet invitations to connect. As participants share their experiences, a communal bond forms, each person learning not only from their own observations but from the insights of others, deepening their understanding of how fairies communicate.

Respect for boundaries is essential in sharing fairy wisdom, as fairies are sensitive to the intentions and openness of each seeker. The practitioner emphasizes the importance of approaching fairies without expectation, allowing relationships to unfold naturally. Each participant is reminded that fairies are beings of free will, and any connection must be reciprocal and mutually respected. The practitioner teaches that just as one would approach a wild animal with gentle respect, so must one approach fairies—with humility, patience, and a willingness to listen. Fairies reveal themselves when they sense that their presence will be honored, and the practitioner's role is to impart this understanding, helping participants cultivate a respectful attitude toward these beings.

As part of the session, participants may engage in a "quiet offering ritual" to express gratitude for the fairies' presence. Each person is given a small token—a leaf, a stone, or a flower—to place on the altar or within a natural space, a gesture that signifies appreciation. The practitioner invites each participant to speak a simple phrase of gratitude, such as, "Thank you, fairies of the land, for your guidance and presence," creating a shared moment of connection and respect. This act of offering, while small, holds deep meaning, as fairies recognize these gestures as affirmations of the bond being cultivated.

To conclude, the practitioner guides a short reflection session, encouraging each participant to share their experience, insights, or any feelings that emerged during the gathering. This open sharing honors each person's unique perspective, reinforcing the idea that fairy wisdom is both universal and deeply personal. As participants express their reflections, the practitioner listens, acknowledging that each story, each connection, is a sacred addition to the collective understanding of fairies. In this moment, the shared wisdom creates a communal space where each participant, whether experienced or new, is both learner and teacher, held in a circle of mutual respect and curiosity.

The session closes with a final moment of gratitude and grounding, as the practitioner leads a soft-spoken farewell to the fairies, releasing their energy with the same respect with which it was welcomed. The group may place their hands over their hearts, silently thanking the fairies for their guidance, and sending a respectful wish that their own paths continue in harmony with the fairy realm. As participants leave, they carry with them not only the knowledge shared but also a heightened sense of presence, an awareness of fairies as both guardians and companions in life's journey.

Through this practice, the practitioner learns that sharing fairy wisdom is less about transferring knowledge and more about inspiring connection, awakening the sense of wonder and respect that invites fairies into one's life. Each gathering, each story, becomes a seed, planted with the intention of fostering relationships built on balance, harmony, and reverence for the unseen. In sharing fairy wisdom, the practitioner joins a timeless tradition, becoming part of the web of nature's teachings, where each soul touched by fairy magic becomes a guardian of its presence in the world.

As the practitioner's understanding of fairy wisdom deepens, so too does their role as a guide for others on this path. Sharing wisdom in a way that honors both the fairies and each unique seeker requires sensitivity, intuition, and a structured approach that allows each participant to find their own connection. In these gatherings, the practitioner not only teaches but also facilitates experiences where fairy energy can be felt, understood, and respected. Through these practices, participants are gently encouraged to explore their own spiritual journey with fairies, fostering a community that celebrates and respects the sacred.

To open these advanced gatherings, the practitioner may create a focused circle, drawing everyone into a shared space of intention and harmony. This circle is a symbolic container for the wisdom shared and received, setting a tone of unity and balance. At the center, an altar serves as a point of focus, adorned with natural elements representing each of the four directions—earth, water, fire, and air. Stones, water bowls, candles, and feathers invite the presence of fairies, signaling that this gathering is held with respect and reverence. By beginning in this structured, intentional way, the practitioner creates an environment that feels sacred and welcoming, a space where fairies may feel inclined to join.

An advanced teaching technique, known as "guided visualization," introduces participants to deeper layers of fairy connection. As the practitioner leads the group in a quiet visualization, each person is invited to enter an inner landscape—a forest, a meadow, or a riverbank—where they may encounter the subtle presence of fairies. Through gentle, descriptive guidance, the practitioner describes sensory details—the warmth of the sun, the texture of the earth, the sounds of nature—drawing each person into a vivid experience that resonates with the fairy realm. In this meditative state, participants are encouraged to listen, to feel, and to trust any impressions or sensations that arise. Each visualization becomes a personal encounter, an opportunity for participants to sense fairy energy in a way that feels intimate and meaningful.

Following the visualization, participants are given time to journal their experiences, capturing insights, feelings, and any subtle signs they may have sensed. This journaling process is encouraged as a way to honor and remember the fairy connection, a record of each unique journey into the world of unseen energies. By writing down these reflections, participants create a bridge between the meditative and the tangible, deepening their understanding and appreciation of fairy presence. The practitioner may gently encourage participants to trust their impressions, explaining that fairies often communicate through intuition and feeling, offering gentle nudges rather than clear answers.

To strengthen each person's personal connection, the practitioner introduces a practice known as "fairy offerings," an act that expresses gratitude and establishes reciprocity with fairies. Participants are invited to create simple tokens of thanks—perhaps a small pouch filled with herbs, flowers, or a handwritten note of gratitude. These offerings, crafted with mindfulness, symbolize each person's appreciation for the fairies' guidance and support. When placed upon the altar or left in nature, these tokens resonate with the fairies, as they sense the sincerity and respect imbued in each offering. This practice not only invites fairy presence but reminds participants of the importance of giving and receiving in their relationship with the unseen world.

As the gathering progresses, the practitioner introduces methods for interpreting signs and synchronicities, a vital skill in understanding the subtle ways fairies communicate. Through guided discussion, participants are encouraged to reflect on recurring symbols, dreams, or natural signs they may encounter. The practitioner explains that fairies, attuned to cycles and patterns, often communicate through repeated signs—perhaps a particular bird appearing frequently, an unexpected feather, or a series of similar dreams. By sharing personal experiences and discussing interpretations, participants learn to discern and trust these subtle communications, developing a deeper awareness of how fairies guide and affirm their path.

To foster group unity and shared learning, the practitioner introduces a collaborative exercise called "circle storytelling."

Each participant takes turns sharing a personal experience, observation, or insight related to fairies, allowing the group to build upon each other's understanding. As stories are shared, a sense of communal wisdom emerges, with each person contributing to a collective tapestry of fairy knowledge. This storytelling not only strengthens the bonds within the group but also invites fairies to linger in the gathering, as they are often drawn to genuine, heartfelt exchanges. Participants find that by listening to each other, they receive insights and perspectives that deepen their own connection with fairies, as if the fairies themselves are speaking through the collective experience.

In addition to personal stories, the practitioner may introduce "fairy-inspired rituals" that participants can practice independently or within their own communities. These simple rituals—such as lighting a candle at dusk, planting a tree in gratitude, or meditating by water—are accessible yet profound acts of connection. Each ritual honors the cycles and elements fairies cherish, creating a rhythm of practice that aligns with fairy energy. By sharing these rituals, the practitioner empowers participants to carry fairy wisdom into their daily lives, cultivating a personal practice that enriches and sustains their bond with fairies.

As the session nears its close, the practitioner leads a shared gratitude ritual, an expression of appreciation for both the fairies and each participant's contributions. Each person may be invited to place their hand on their heart and silently thank the fairies for their guidance, or to offer a few words of thanks aloud. A small bowl of water or earth may be passed around, each participant taking a moment to place a finger within, symbolizing their connection to nature and the fairies' world. These gestures, while simple, resonate deeply within the group, reinforcing a sense of unity, respect, and shared purpose.

The practitioner closes the gathering by releasing the fairy energy with a gentle invocation, such as, "Fairies of nature and guardians of balance, we thank you for your presence and wisdom. May our paths remain open to your guidance, and may we honor your gifts in all that we do." This closing acknowledgment, spoken with humility, completes the circle, signaling to the fairies that the session is concluded with respect. Participants are encouraged to leave quietly, carrying with them a sense of stillness and connection, each person reminded of the fairies' enduring presence in the world around them.

In the days that follow, participants often find that their sensitivity to fairy energy increases, noticing small yet significant changes—a heightened awareness of natural patterns, a renewed appreciation for quiet moments, or a growing understanding of how fairies communicate through signs. The fairies, sensing the openness and respect cultivated in these gatherings, may choose to reveal themselves more readily, responding to each participant's unique spirit and dedication.

Through these gatherings, the practitioner becomes not only a guide but a guardian of fairy wisdom, helping others to weave the presence of fairies into their own lives with reverence and joy. Each session, each shared story, becomes a thread in a tapestry of connection, a living legacy of wisdom passed from soul to soul. The fairies, ever sensitive to intention and respect, respond to these gatherings with a quiet, gentle presence, knowing that their guidance will continue to ripple outward, touching each participant's life in unseen yet profound ways.

By creating these circles of shared experience, the practitioner fulfills a role of sacred stewardship, ensuring that fairy wisdom is not only preserved but celebrated and shared. Each person who leaves the circle carries a spark of this wisdom into the world, a reminder of the fairies' timeless guidance and the beauty of living in harmony with nature's hidden realms.

Chapter 12
Energy Awareness

Awakening to the subtle energies that weave through the natural world is like discovering a new language—one that the fairies, as keepers of this energy, understand intimately. Energy awareness is the practice of perceiving these unseen forces and recognizing how they shape our lives and environments.

The first step in developing energy awareness is grounding, a process that connects one's energy to the earth, creating a stable foundation from which sensitivity can grow. The practitioner begins by standing barefoot on the ground, taking deep, measured breaths, and visualizing roots extending from their feet deep into the earth. This connection with the earth's energy stabilizes the practitioner's own field, aligning it with the fairies' rhythms. Grounding provides the practitioner with a centered awareness, a calm receptiveness that allows subtle energies to become more noticeable. Fairies, ever watchful of those who align themselves with nature, often sense this grounded presence and may approach more readily, recognizing an openness and respect for their world.

From this foundation, the practitioner moves to an exercise called "energy scanning." This practice teaches how to sense energy with the hands, allowing the practitioner to feel variations in temperature, pressure, or vibration that indicate shifts in the surrounding energy. With palms facing each other, just a few inches apart, the practitioner slowly moves their hands closer and then further apart, becoming aware of any tingling, warmth, or resistance between them. This sensation, often described as a "magnetic" pull or gentle resistance, is the first sign of energy awareness. Practicing this exercise daily, the practitioner develops a heightened sense of touch, learning to recognize the unique sensations that indicate the presence of energy, whether it's from the earth, an object, or the fairies themselves.

Fairies, sensitive to energy, often reveal themselves through gentle shifts in the atmosphere. Thus, the practitioner may extend their energy awareness to natural settings, such as forests, riversides, or gardens, where fairy presence is strong. The practice of "nature tuning" is a simple yet profound way to sense fairy energy. Sitting quietly outdoors, the practitioner allows their awareness to expand, feeling the life in the trees, the flow of the wind, and the rhythm of birdsong. With each breath, they draw in the energy of the place, letting it fill their senses until they can feel the subtle differences in each area. Fairies, who are deeply attuned to these landscapes, often make their presence known through subtle signs, such as a sudden rustling of leaves, a warmth in the air, or the feeling of being gently watched.

Another exercise, known as "elemental attunement," focuses on perceiving the unique qualities of earth, air, fire, and water, which are the primary elements that fairies embody and protect. In this exercise, the practitioner selects a natural object that corresponds to each element—a stone for earth, a feather for air, a candle for fire, and a small bowl of water. By holding each object in turn, they close their eyes, focusing on the sensations, images, or emotions that arise. Holding a stone, for example, might evoke a feeling of solidity and stability, while a feather might bring lightness and openness. Through repeated practice, the practitioner becomes more adept at sensing the individual qualities of each element, building a sensitivity that mirrors the fairies' own understanding of these forces.

As sensitivity grows, so does the ability to sense shifts in energy within familiar environments. Fairies often leave traces of their presence, an "energetic imprint" that remains in places they frequent. The practice of "energy mapping" allows the practitioner to identify these subtle changes in their home or outdoor spaces. Walking slowly through each area, they pause and extend their awareness, feeling for any areas of warmth, coolness, or movement that feel different from the rest. Often, these places are near plants, windows, or natural elements that fairies favor, such as stones or flowers. By identifying these imprints, the practitioner learns to recognize spaces that resonate with fairy energy, understanding where the fairies may be more inclined to linger.

Throughout these exercises, breathing remains a crucial tool for connecting to the flow of energy. The practitioner learns a technique called "breath awareness," which involves breathing slowly and intentionally while focusing on the sensations within the body. By bringing attention to each inhale and exhale, they become attuned to the energy shifts within themselves, creating a state of calm receptiveness. This practice allows for a balanced exchange between the practitioner's energy and the energies surrounding them, a resonance that fairies often respond to with subtle presence. Each breath becomes an invitation, a gesture that says, "I am here, listening, ready to connect."

As the practitioner's awareness grows, they may begin to notice "energy pulses"—fleeting sensations that arise unexpectedly, like a warm breeze, a faint tingle on the skin, or a sense of gentle pressure in the air. Fairies, who communicate through these currents, often use these pulses to signal their presence or respond to the practitioner's awareness. Over time, the practitioner learns to distinguish between ordinary environmental changes and these intentional signals, developing a language of feeling that allows for quiet, intuitive conversations with the fairies.

The practice of energy awareness is a journey of patience and dedication. By building sensitivity to the subtle energies in everyday life, the practitioner enters into a state of mindfulness that aligns with the fairies' way of being. Each moment of attunement, whether in nature or at home, becomes a chance to honor the energies that surround all things, recognizing them as alive, interconnected, and sacred. Through these quiet practices, the practitioner discovers that fairy presence is not so much a rare occurrence as a constant, quiet companionship—an ever-present whisper of nature's energy flowing through each day.

In this gentle opening of awareness, the practitioner learns that energy is not static but a dynamic and responsive field, one that shifts and changes with intention, emotion, and thought. Fairies, ever observant, recognize this dedication and often respond by deepening the connection, fostering a bond of mutual respect. As this bond strengthens, the practitioner finds that energy awareness becomes second nature, a part of every moment, and that the fairy realm is no longer distant but intertwined with their daily life, like a melody that hums just beneath the surface.

Through energy awareness, the practitioner awakens to a deeper understanding of themselves and the world, perceiving life as a continuous exchange of presence and spirit. In this state, they walk with fairies in a quiet partnership, embracing a life enriched by a new sensitivity, where each breath, each moment of stillness, becomes an invitation to connect with the energies that sustain and shape the world around them.

As the journey of energy awareness deepens, the practitioner learns to refine their sensitivity, perceiving energy as more than mere sensations but as a nuanced language that speaks of connection, intention, and presence.

To enhance this understanding, the practitioner begins by exploring "energy texture," a technique that allows them to identify the different qualities of energy they encounter. By using their hands to scan an object or space, they focus on discerning whether the energy feels warm, cool, dense, or light. These textures are not random; they reflect the characteristics of the energies present. For instance, dense, warm energy often suggests a grounding, protective force, while light, cool energy may indicate the influence of fairies associated with air or water. By becoming familiar with these textures, the practitioner learns to interpret the subtle distinctions that reveal the presence and nature of fairy energies.

The practice of "dynamic attunement" then guides the practitioner to recognize how energy shifts in response to various intentions and moods. Fairies, who are acutely sensitive to human emotions, may respond differently depending on the practitioner's state of mind. For example, when the practitioner approaches with a calm, open heart, fairy energy often feels inviting and warm, while moments of stress or haste may evoke a cooler, more reserved response. The practitioner begins each day with a few moments of reflection, noting their own emotional state and observing how the energy around them responds. By becoming mindful of these shifts, they learn to approach the fairies with an energy of respect and calm, fostering a deeper connection through intentional alignment.

In addition to observing their own energy, the practitioner explores how environmental energy varies with time and natural cycles. The practice of "cyclic awareness" involves tuning in to the subtle shifts that accompany dawn, dusk, and seasonal transitions, times when fairy energy is particularly active. Each cycle brings a unique quality to the energy of a place—the freshness of morning, the stillness of dusk, the quiet depth of winter, or the vibrant growth of spring. By immersing themselves in these moments, the practitioner becomes attuned to the natural ebb and flow of energy, sensing when fairy presence is strongest and understanding how to align their practices with these rhythms for heightened connection.

This sensitivity is deepened further through "resonance listening," a technique in which the practitioner learns to recognize the frequencies at which different energies resonate. Just as sounds have distinct pitches and tones, energies vibrate at different frequencies, which can be subtly perceived by the practitioner's body. Fairies, who exist at a higher vibrational frequency than most physical energies, often appear as a gentle tingling or a light buzzing sensation. By tuning into this resonance, the practitioner distinguishes fairy energy from other presences, allowing for a clearer and more focused connection. With practice, they begin to recognize the "signature" of each fairy's energy, much like a familiar melody that resonates uniquely with each encounter.

To further refine energy awareness, the practitioner may also use a technique called "energy anchoring." This involves focusing on a specific point within the body, such as the heart or solar plexus, and visualizing it as a stable center that receives and processes the surrounding energy. By anchoring awareness in this way, the practitioner creates a focal point that stabilizes their own energy while allowing them to observe external energies without becoming overwhelmed. This anchored state fosters a calm receptiveness, where the practitioner can clearly sense the fairies' presence without interference from fluctuating emotions or environmental distractions. Fairies recognize this stability and often draw closer, sensing a respectful openness that allows for deeper interactions.

With this refined sensitivity, the practitioner is now prepared to engage in a practice known as "energy merging." This technique involves consciously blending one's own energy with the energies of the environment, opening a pathway to experience the world as the fairies do. To begin, the practitioner sits quietly, focusing on their breath and visualizing themselves as a part of the landscape—a tree, a river, or even the earth itself. With each inhale, they draw in the energy of their surroundings, and with each exhale, they release any separation, merging with the landscape. This merging creates a state of oneness, where the boundaries between self and environment dissolve. In this state, the practitioner experiences a profound alignment with nature, sensing the fairies' perspective as guardians of these energies and understanding how deeply they are intertwined with the elements.

Fairies, sensing the practitioner's openness, may respond to this merging by enhancing the experience with their own energy. The practitioner may feel an increase in warmth, lightness, or even a gentle stirring in the air—signs that the fairies are harmonizing with the practitioner's energy field. This merging fosters a bond that goes beyond physical perception; it is an invitation to understand life through the fairies' perspective, where every element, from the smallest pebble to the vast sky, holds significance and purpose. Through this union, the practitioner gains insight into the interconnectedness of all things, a wisdom that the fairies, with their timeless knowledge, embody fully.

The final practice, "intuitive energy mapping," allows the practitioner to visualize and interpret the patterns of energy they encounter, forming a mental map that guides future interactions. By standing in a chosen environment, they close their eyes and envision the energy flow around them—seeing it as light, color, or even sound. Patterns emerge: areas where energy feels dense, places where it flows freely, or pockets that seem to hum with fairy presence. This mapping not only helps the practitioner recognize areas where fairies dwell but also reveals how to adjust their own energy to harmonize with these patterns. With time, this practice teaches the practitioner to navigate energy landscapes intuitively, fostering a natural ease in their interactions with fairies and the energies they protect.

As this journey of energy awareness unfolds, the practitioner discovers that each technique, each layer of sensitivity, brings them closer to the fairies' world. The fairies, noticing this dedication, often respond by revealing themselves more openly, sometimes through subtle signs, such as a unique flower, a particularly vivid dream, or an unusual bird call. These signs affirm the growing partnership, reminding the practitioner that their efforts to honor and understand energy are seen and appreciated.

With this level of awareness, the practitioner becomes not just a visitor to the fairy realm but an active participant, someone who lives in harmony with the unseen energies that surround and sustain all things. Each day, each interaction with nature becomes an opportunity to deepen this relationship, to walk with the fairies not only as guides but as companions in a shared journey of balance, respect, and reverence.

Chapter 13
Renewal Rituals

In moments when life's demands drain vitality or when inner balance feels disrupted, fairies—guardians of nature's cycles—offer guidance through the power of renewal. Renewal rituals are sacred practices that invite the fairies' energy to cleanse, revitalize, and restore harmony within oneself and one's surroundings. These rituals honor the fairies as beings attuned to the ebb and flow of life, celebrating their role in rejuvenating both the spirit and environment. By working alongside fairies, the practitioner learns to tap into this restorative energy, clearing away stagnant influences and making space for new growth and vibrancy.

To begin, the practitioner prepares by clearing both mind and space, creating an environment where renewal energy can flow unimpeded. This initial clearing is done with intention, signaling to the fairies that a ritual of purification and rebirth is about to unfold. Burning herbs such as sage, lavender, or cedar, the practitioner gently wafts the smoke through each corner of the room, setting an intention for the space to be cleansed of any residual energies. The fairies, sensitive to scents and natural elements, recognize these signals, often responding with subtle signs—a shift in temperature, a lightness in the air, or the sense of calm that fills the room.

The first step in personal renewal is grounding, a foundational exercise that connects the practitioner's energy to the earth. Standing with feet firmly on the ground, the practitioner visualizes roots extending downward, reaching deep into the soil, absorbing the stabilizing energy of the earth. Each inhale draws in this grounding force, each exhale releases tension, stress, and anything that no longer serves. This grounding aligns the practitioner with the earth's own cycles, creating a stable foundation upon which renewal can occur. Fairies connected to the earth element often lend their presence during this process, providing a sense of rootedness and calm that enhances the ritual's effectiveness.

With grounding established, the practitioner moves into "energy cleansing," a practice of releasing accumulated negative or stagnant energy. Holding a crystal known for purification, such as clear quartz or selenite, the practitioner breathes deeply, visualizing a soft, white light flowing through the body, cleansing every cell, every thought, every emotion. This light, symbolizing the fairies' gentle and renewing energy, moves through the practitioner, carrying away all that no longer resonates with their current state of being. As the practitioner visualizes this energy flowing out, they may feel a lightness or a release, an indication that the fairies are supporting this act of purification, carrying away any energies that weigh down the spirit.

To further enhance the cleansing process, a "water renewal ritual" is introduced, using the element most associated with purification and emotional release. The practitioner fills a bowl with pure water, adding a few drops of essential oil, such as eucalyptus or rosemary, known for their cleansing properties. They dip their fingers into the water, closing their eyes and inviting the water fairies to bless the ritual. With each drop that touches the skin, the practitioner imagines layers of stagnant energy washing away, leaving them refreshed and renewed. The water absorbs this energy, symbolizing a release from emotional burdens. Afterward, the water is respectfully returned to the earth, allowing nature to transform and purify these energies, completing the cycle of renewal.

In the final phase, the practitioner invites a flow of rejuvenating energy to fill the space cleared through cleansing. This step, known as "energy replenishment," involves calling upon the fairies to lend their vibrant, restorative presence. Seated quietly, the practitioner visualizes themselves bathed in a soft, radiant light—green for the vitality of earth fairies, blue for the soothing energy of water fairies, or golden for the warmth of fire fairies. This light fills every part of their being, revitalizing and restoring a sense of well-being and harmony. The fairies, recognizing the practitioner's openness to renewal, often respond with a gentle surge of energy, a sign that they are actively supporting this ritual of transformation.

Fairies honor the act of renewal, as it mirrors their own nature—the continuous cycle of life, death, and rebirth that maintains balance in the natural world. Through these renewal rituals, the practitioner learns to embrace change, recognizing that release and replenishment are essential to personal growth. The presence of fairies during these rituals brings a sense of peace and clarity, a reminder that renewal is not only a physical or mental practice but a spiritual alignment with the natural cycles that sustain life. With each ritual, the practitioner becomes more attuned to these rhythms, finding solace in the quiet transformation that follows each act of cleansing and replenishment.

By embracing these practices, the practitioner discovers that renewal rituals are not only for moments of depletion but can be integrated into regular cycles, allowing the spirit to remain resilient and open to life's changes. As fairies assist in these rituals, they teach that true renewal lies not in resisting change but in flowing with it, accepting the natural process of releasing the old to make room for the new. Through these sacred practices, the practitioner learns that with each breath, each choice, each intention, renewal is a constant presence, a quiet reminder that harmony lies within the cycles that the fairies so lovingly protect.

With the groundwork of renewal rituals established, the practitioner can now deepen this journey, exploring more refined techniques that harness the fairies' energies to revitalize and transform. These advanced practices go beyond personal renewal, offering ways to channel renewal energy for specific intentions—such as creative inspiration, emotional healing, or environmental harmony. Guided by the fairies, the practitioner learns that renewal is not a singular act but a continuous flow that refreshes all aspects of life, connecting them to the ever-evolving cycles of nature.

One profound method to expand renewal rituals is the "circle of replenishment," a sacred technique that creates a sphere of revitalizing energy within the chosen ritual space. To form this circle, the practitioner begins by placing symbols of each element at four points around the space—earth to the north, air to the east, fire to the south, and water to the west. These symbols may be a small stone, a feather, a candle, and a bowl of water. Standing at the center, the practitioner calls upon fairies associated with each element, asking them to bless the space with their renewing essence. As the fairies respond, the practitioner may sense an energy shift, a subtle glow, or a warmth that signifies their presence.

With the elements aligned, the practitioner visualizes energy flowing from each point, creating a continuous circle that surrounds the space in a sphere of light. This energy, a blend of earth's stability, air's clarity, fire's vitality, and water's calm, forms a powerful field that promotes renewal on multiple levels. The fairies, guardians of these elements, naturally harmonize the circle's flow, refining and enhancing the energy's quality. In this sphere, the practitioner feels a profound sense of balance and grounding, each element in harmony, each aspect of their spirit renewed and refreshed. This "circle of replenishment" can remain active as long as needed, providing a sanctuary of energy that nurtures and restores anyone within its bounds.

To amplify this renewal, the practitioner may engage in the practice of "elemental breathing," focusing on drawing in the unique energy of each element through breath. Inhaling deeply, they visualize drawing earth energy from below, feeling its steady, grounding influence fortify the body. Next, breathing in air from all around, they absorb clarity and openness, freeing the mind of tension. Fire energy, inhaled as warmth and vitality, energizes the spirit, while water, visualized as a cooling flow, soothes and refreshes the emotional body. By cycling through each element in turn, the practitioner brings balance to every level of their being, harmonizing with the fairies' essence that lives within these forces. Each breath becomes an act of renewal, a rhythm that flows with the fairies' own understanding of life's constant evolution.

As the practitioner explores these layers of renewal, "visualization of blossoming" serves as a powerful technique to direct this energy toward personal goals or creative inspiration. Seated within the circle of replenishment, they visualize a budding flower in the center of their heart, symbolizing an intention or area of life where renewal is desired. With each breath, they imagine the flower slowly opening, its petals unfurling as the energy of renewal flows into it. This unfolding represents the gradual, nurturing process of growth, a reminder that true renewal is not instant but cultivated over time. Fairies, whose presence often feels like the unfolding of nature itself, support this blossoming, adding a touch of their own vibrant energy to the process. The practitioner feels this support as a gentle warmth or sense of encouragement, a subtle push toward new beginnings and creative expression.

In addition to personal renewal, the practitioner learns to apply these techniques in service of environmental harmony. Through "environmental renewal," they extend the fairies' energy to spaces that may feel stagnant or unbalanced, such as a room in the home or a section of the garden. Standing in the chosen area, the practitioner calls upon the fairies, asking for their guidance in restoring harmony. With hands extended, they visualize drawing in the fairies' renewing energy, seeing it as a shimmering light that fills the space. This light, infused with the essence of renewal, gently shifts and clears any lingering energies, revitalizing the area with the fairies' presence. Often, subtle signs—such as a fresh breeze, a sudden sense of calm, or the gentle appearance of natural life—signal that the fairies have responded, transforming the environment into a place of peace and vibrancy.

Another technique, "offering of seeds," symbolizes a commitment to renewal not only for oneself but for the earth. This ritual honors the fairies' role in nature's cycle, mirroring their dedication to the nurturing of life. The practitioner selects seeds from plants known for their resilience and regenerative properties—such as lavender, sage, or wildflowers. With each seed held in the hand, they offer a silent blessing, imbuing it with intentions of renewal and growth. Planted in the earth with respect, these seeds carry both the practitioner's and the fairies' energies, becoming physical manifestations of the commitment to renewal. Over time, as these seeds grow, they embody the spirit of renewal, a living testament to the fairies' guidance and the practitioner's dedication to harmonizing with nature's rhythms.

To conclude the advanced renewal ritual, the practitioner practices "silent gratitude," a closing that honors both the fairies and the energies they've received. Seated quietly, hands placed gently over the heart, they bring to mind each aspect of the ritual—the cleansing, the circle of replenishment, the elements, and the fairies who were present. Inwardly, they express gratitude, sending a silent wave of appreciation to the fairies for their assistance and to the elements for their support. This act of gratitude reinforces the connection, recognizing renewal as a gift that is sustained through respect and intention. The fairies, sensing this sincerity, often leave a sign of acknowledgment—a sense of warmth, a fleeting scent of flowers, or a feeling of lightness—as a subtle affirmation of the shared journey.

Through these advanced renewal rituals, the practitioner comes to understand that renewal is not merely a process but a way of being. It is a commitment to align with life's natural flow, to honor the fairies' role as keepers of balance, and to recognize that every end is a new beginning. Each ritual, each breath, becomes part of a greater cycle that sustains not only the practitioner but the world around them. This awareness brings a quiet resilience, an understanding that renewal is always available, a gentle pulse of life that the fairies help guide and sustain.

In this partnership with the fairies, the practitioner learns to live with grace and adaptability, finding strength in renewal's quiet, nurturing power. The fairies, guardians of these sacred cycles, continue to guide, their presence a reminder that life's beauty lies in its capacity for constant, gentle transformation. Through these practices, the practitioner carries the fairies' wisdom forward, living each day with an open heart, ready to release, renew, and grow in harmony with the timeless rhythm of the earth.

Chapter 14
Self-Love Ritual

As the practitioner's journey with fairies deepens, the exploration of self-love emerges as a natural and essential part of spiritual growth. Self-love, as the fairies gently teach, is not simply an appreciation of oneself but a commitment to nurturing and honoring the inner spirit. Fairies, who are guardians of nature's harmony, recognize that true love for oneself creates a balanced foundation from which all other relationships flourish. Through the self-love ritual, the practitioner learns to open their heart to the gentle presence of fairies, inviting their energy to help cultivate compassion, kindness, and respect for one's own being.

The self-love ritual begins with creating a space that reflects the fairies' essence of warmth and acceptance. Soft candlelight, petals scattered across the altar, and a soothing fragrance of roses or lavender set a tone of calm and beauty, mirroring the gentle presence fairies embody. This atmosphere, filled with elements that encourage a peaceful mindset, allows the practitioner to step into a space of openness and receptivity. The practitioner invites the fairies to join, signaling that this is a moment dedicated to healing and nurturing the self. Fairies often respond to such invitations with a quiet, comforting energy, their presence a reminder of the simplicity and beauty of self-compassion.

To begin, the practitioner places a hand on their heart, closing their eyes and taking slow, deep breaths. This gentle focus on the heart center becomes a grounding point, creating a connection to the inner self where self-love resides. The breath, a rhythmic flow, acts as a calming guide, quieting any distractions and bringing the practitioner fully into the present moment. In this space, they allow any emotions—tenderness, sorrow, joy, or longing—to surface naturally, knowing that fairies are near, offering support without judgment. This practice, a simple act of presence, is an acknowledgment of the self, an invitation to explore what lies within with kindness.

The next step introduces a visualization known as the "rose of self-compassion." The practitioner imagines a rose blooming at the center of their heart, each petal unfolding softly, symbolizing layers of self-love that are waiting to be embraced. With each breath, the rose opens further, a beautiful and vibrant symbol of their own worth and uniqueness. The fairies, who often connect through symbols of nature, may make their presence felt as a warm or tingling sensation near the heart, amplifying the experience of this unfolding. As the rose blooms, the practitioner silently affirms phrases of love and kindness, such as "I am worthy," "I am enough," or "I honor my journey." Each affirmation is an expression of self-love that resonates with the fairies' energy, creating a harmony that strengthens the bond between them and the practitioner.

After nurturing this sense of self-compassion, the practitioner moves to a practice called "mirroring." In this exercise, they look into a mirror placed on the altar, gazing gently into their own reflection. This moment of self-observation is not about judgment but about seeing oneself with the eyes of compassion and acceptance. With the fairies' energy surrounding them, the practitioner is encouraged to look past any surface insecurities, connecting instead with the spirit within. They might even speak softly to their reflection, offering words of encouragement, love, and forgiveness. This mirror practice, infused with the fairies' gentle support, allows the practitioner to embrace both the strengths and vulnerabilities that make them unique. Through this act, self-love begins to feel tangible, as if the fairies are reminding them that they are, in essence, as much a part of nature as any tree, river, or star.

To deepen the connection, the practitioner engages in a ritual known as "self-embrace." They wrap their arms around themselves, creating a comforting hold, and with closed eyes, focus on the sensation of warmth and safety. This physical act of embracing oneself becomes a powerful gesture of love and acceptance, as if reassuring the inner self that it is cherished and protected. Fairies, who are naturally attuned to gestures of kindness and warmth, often respond to this act with a subtle presence—a whisper of encouragement or a gentle feeling of joy. The practitioner may feel as though they are sharing this embrace with the fairies, a shared moment of gentle, unconditional love.

To close the ritual, the practitioner performs a "heart-offering," placing a small token on the altar as a symbol of their commitment to self-love. This token—perhaps a rose quartz crystal, a handwritten note, or a flower petal—becomes a personal reminder of the journey toward self-acceptance. The practitioner whispers a simple phrase of gratitude, such as, "Thank you, fairies, for reminding me of my own beauty and worth." With this offering, the practitioner acknowledges both their own value and the fairies' role in helping them embrace it. The fairies, sensitive to such moments of sincerity, often respond with a quiet blessing, leaving the practitioner with a lingering sense of warmth and peace.

As the practitioner leaves the space, they carry with them the essence of the ritual—a newfound awareness of self-love that remains present, even in daily life. This self-love, cultivated with the fairies' guidance, becomes a foundation of inner peace, affecting every relationship, every intention, and every action. The fairies, ever watchful and compassionate, continue to support this journey, encouraging the practitioner to honor themselves with the same reverence given to nature's beauty. Through this practice, self-love becomes not only an act of kindness but a path to deeper spiritual growth, one that the fairies joyfully walk alongside.

This journey continues with the practice of "heartlight meditation," a visualization exercise that invites the practitioner to view themselves as a source of radiant love and light. Sitting comfortably, the practitioner places a hand over their heart, breathing deeply, and imagining a soft, warm light emanating from within. This light, symbolizing self-love, expands with each breath, filling the chest and then the entire body, enveloping them in a comforting glow. As the light grows, the practitioner allows it to expand beyond themselves, filling the room with its gentle warmth. Fairies often respond to this light with their own subtle presence, amplifying the energy in a way that feels like a reassuring embrace, a reminder that the practitioner is supported in their journey toward self-love.

With this radiant energy surrounding them, the practitioner may move into "affirmation whispering," an advanced exercise where they repeat affirmations softly, as if sharing them with the fairies. Simple phrases like "I am worthy of love," "I honor my journey," or "I am enough" are spoken in a gentle voice, allowing the words to resonate in the heart and the space around. The fairies, attuned to sound and intention, often join in this practice, magnifying the power of these affirmations with their energy. This exercise becomes a shared expression of love, a conversation where both the practitioner and the fairies affirm a collective belief in the practitioner's inherent worth. Over time, these affirmations take root, subtly transforming the practitioner's self-perception, guiding them to treat themselves with the same kindness they would offer a dear friend.

Building upon this, the practitioner introduces the "mirror of kindness" ritual, where they sit before a mirror and reflect on their own image, exploring self-love through gentle observation. Instead of focusing on perceived flaws, the practitioner is encouraged to see their reflection as a unique expression of spirit and life. By looking deeply, they begin to notice not only physical traits but the warmth and resilience that lies within. With the fairies' energy present, this moment becomes one of honoring the self without judgment, embracing every part of their being as worthy of love and respect. This ritual, practiced over time, encourages the practitioner to view themselves through a lens of kindness, transforming self-perception from one of criticism to one of acceptance.

To deepen the bond between self-love and compassion, the practitioner may perform the "garden of forgiveness," a symbolic ritual that helps release past hurts or regrets that may inhibit self-acceptance. Visualizing an inner garden, the practitioner envisions planting seeds for each aspect of themselves they wish to forgive—perhaps an old regret, a past mistake, or a harsh self-criticism. As these seeds are placed in the soil of the heart, the practitioner whispers a gentle phrase of forgiveness, such as "I release this with love" or "I forgive myself and open to peace." With the fairies' energy nurturing this garden, the seeds begin to grow, symbolizing a release from past burdens and the blossoming of compassion and acceptance. This ritual transforms inner pain into new growth, mirroring the fairies' ability to turn even the smallest spark of life into beauty.

The next step introduces the practice of "receiving love," a guided visualization where the practitioner opens themselves to the fairies' gentle presence as a source of love and support. Sitting quietly, they visualize themselves surrounded by the fairies, feeling their warmth and peaceful energy as a tangible presence. This moment is an invitation for the practitioner to accept love, not as something to be earned but as an inherent right. The fairies, who embody unconditional acceptance, often respond to this invitation by enveloping the practitioner in a comforting sensation—a gentle tingling, warmth, or an inner calm. This practice teaches the practitioner to receive love freely, a reminder that self-love is not only about what one gives to oneself but also about the ability to welcome love from the world around.

With this foundation of acceptance, the practitioner then engages in "self-gratitude journaling," a reflective practice where they write down moments, qualities, or actions for which they are grateful toward themselves. Each entry is a recognition of their efforts, resilience, and kindness—qualities the fairies, too, appreciate in the practitioner. By recording these reflections, they create a tangible record of self-appreciation, a reminder of their unique value and contributions. The fairies, who thrive in moments of gratitude, often bless this practice, infusing the journal with their energy as if each word were a small, precious offering. Over time, this journal becomes a powerful symbol of the practitioner's journey toward self-love, a book that speaks of growth, acceptance, and inner harmony.

To close the ritual, the practitioner performs a "gratitude offering," placing a small gift on the altar—perhaps a flower, a crystal, or a leaf—as an expression of thanks for the fairies' guidance and presence. Whispering words of gratitude, the practitioner honors both themselves and the fairies, recognizing the shared journey toward compassion and love. This offering, made with sincerity, signifies a commitment to self-love and to nurturing this bond with the fairies. The fairies, sensitive to acts of gratitude, may respond with a quiet blessing, a sense of peace that lingers, or a soft, comforting sensation, affirming the practitioner's commitment to inner growth.

As the ritual ends, the practitioner carries with them a deeper understanding of self-love—not as a fleeting feeling, but as a living, breathing practice that shapes their life and spirit. Each affirmation, each moment of forgiveness, and each act of gratitude strengthens the foundation of self-compassion, a bond with the self that the fairies gently encourage and nurture. Through these practices, self-love transforms from a concept into a daily experience, a quiet strength that grows with each breath and every gentle word.

The fairies, who view each soul as inherently beautiful, guide the practitioner to embrace this beauty within. Through these rituals, the practitioner learns that self-love is a journey that unfolds with patience and care, a path where kindness and compassion are as essential as light and water to a growing plant. With each step, each ritual, the practitioner walks closer to a life lived in harmony with themselves and the fairies, honoring the quiet, enduring love that lies at the heart of all things.

Chapter 15
Communication with Nature

In the quiet spaces of nature, where sunlight filters through leaves, and rivers sing softly over stones, the fairies move as stewards of the earth's wisdom. Communication with nature is a journey of attunement, a subtle conversation that allows the practitioner to connect deeply with both the fairy realm and the elements.

To open this practice, the practitioner prepares by entering a natural space, perhaps a forest, meadow, or even a small garden. Standing quietly, they close their eyes and take a few deep breaths, allowing the mind to quiet and the senses to expand. This state of mindfulness becomes the foundation for deeper connection, creating a stillness that the fairies recognize and respond to. By aligning themselves with the natural world in this way, the practitioner opens an invisible door, inviting fairies and the spirits of nature to communicate. In the fairies' realm, a quiet mind and an open heart are the truest invitations.

The first practice, "elemental sensing," introduces the practitioner to the subtle energies of each element present in their surroundings—earth, water, air, and the warmth of sunlight, which connects with fire. Moving slowly, they touch the earth with their hands, feeling the steady presence beneath, which resonates with the fairies who protect and nourish the soil. By placing their hands near a flowing stream or fountain, they connect to the fluid, adaptive energy of water, which fairies often use to carry messages of flow and change. Inhaling deeply, they breathe in the air, sensing its lightness and freedom, and finally, feel the sun's warmth, a reminder of life's vitality and renewal. This sensory practice builds a rapport with each element, a fundamental step in understanding the fairies' world, which is interwoven with these forces. Through repeated practice, the practitioner begins to discern the unique language of each element, a silent conversation that fairies use to share their guidance.

With this foundation, the practitioner is ready to engage in "listening to the whispers," a technique that deepens their sensitivity to subtle sounds and shifts in the natural environment. Standing quietly, they focus on each sound around them—the rustling of leaves, the soft hum of insects, the distant call of birds. Instead of interpreting these as random noises, they learn to perceive them as messages, part of the fairies' way of communicating through nature. The fairies often use small signs, like a sudden rustling or the song of a bird at just the right moment, to affirm their presence. With time, the practitioner begins to recognize the patterns in these sounds, sensing which may hold particular meaning. Each whisper, each note, becomes a reminder of the fairies' watchful, guiding presence.

Another layer of communication unfolds through the practice of "symbolic sight," where the practitioner becomes attuned to natural symbols that the fairies use to convey messages. Walking slowly through a natural setting, they observe with heightened awareness, noticing leaves that form patterns, stones that seem to shine with unexpected light, or flowers that appear in unusual places. Each of these natural symbols is a form of language, a quiet message from the fairies. A butterfly landing nearby, a feather on the path, or a cluster of mushrooms—each symbol holds a meaning unique to the practitioner's journey. The fairies use these signs to nudge the practitioner, guiding them to understand nature as a living tapestry of wisdom and support.

For a more direct form of communication, the practitioner engages in "nature journaling," a practice where they record observations, sensations, and symbolic encounters. Sitting comfortably, they open a journal and begin to write down the details of their experience—whether it's the way sunlight fell through the trees, the sound of a nearby brook, or a particularly strong sense of peace in a specific area. This journal becomes a bridge between the practitioner and the fairies, a place where they capture subtle messages that might otherwise be overlooked. Over time, patterns and insights emerge in these entries, revealing the ways in which nature communicates personally and directly with them. The fairies, aware of the practitioner's dedication to listening, often respond by making their presence more apparent, adding depth to the journal's entries and meanings.

The final practice, "energy merging with nature," invites the practitioner to experience a deeper level of communication, where they blend their own energy with the landscape. Seated on the ground, they close their eyes and visualize their energy extending outward, merging gently with the earth, trees, and sky. In this state of oneness, they feel their own rhythm align with nature's pulse, sensing the fairies' presence as part of this larger energy field. This merging fosters an awareness that transcends words, a felt sense of communion with the world around. The fairies, drawn to those who honor the interconnectedness of life, often respond by amplifying the practitioner's sensitivity, creating a moment of unity where the self and the natural world flow as one.

As the practitioner grows familiar with these practices, communication with nature becomes a natural, intuitive experience—a quiet understanding that exists beyond words. They begin to walk through forests, gardens, or mountains with a heightened sense of presence, knowing that each step, each breath, is part of an ongoing conversation with the fairies. Every leaf, every ripple of water, and every whisper of wind holds the potential for connection, a reminder that the fairies' world is close, accessible to those who listen with open hearts.

Through this journey, the practitioner discovers that nature is not separate from themselves but a part of their inner being, a mirror to the spirit. The fairies, who reside in the smallest flowers and the tallest trees, guide them to see that nature's beauty is not only external but a reflection of their own spirit. This understanding, cultivated through the gentle art of listening, transforms the practitioner's relationship with the world around them. It becomes a relationship of respect, gratitude, and quiet joy—a connection that enriches both spirit and soul, as the fairies watch over, guiding with every subtle touch of the natural world.

As the practitioner's ability to communicate with nature deepens, so does their awareness of the fairies' subtle yet profound guidance. In this expanded journey, the practitioner learns to go beyond initial impressions, exploring a richer connection where signs and sensations become a two-way conversation with the natural world.

To begin this advanced exploration, the practitioner engages in "energy attunement walks," a method of synchronizing their energy with the environment in a way that enhances sensitivity. During these walks, they move slowly, attuned to each step, each breath, and each sensation. Instead of merely observing, they bring their awareness to the way their body feels in different areas—how the atmosphere may feel lighter near a grove of trees or how a particular stone radiates warmth. Fairies often use these subtle shifts in energy to communicate, guiding the practitioner toward areas rich with presence or significance. This practice develops a sense of spatial awareness, where each part of the landscape becomes infused with layers of meaning, deepening the relationship with the fairies and their habitat.

An advanced practice called "nature meditation with the elements" then guides the practitioner to connect individually with earth, water, air, and fire within the natural environment. For this, they select a quiet location and find a place to sit near representations of each element—a tree or stone for earth, a flowing stream or even a small water bowl for water, an open sky for air, and the warmth of sunlight or a small flame for fire. Sitting in this elemental circle, the practitioner meditates on each element's unique qualities and how they resonate within. The fairies often draw near during this exercise, enhancing the practitioner's awareness with sensations—such as a warmth that isn't from the sun or a breeze that seems to carry a gentle message. By meditating with each element in turn, the practitioner strengthens their connection with both the natural world and the fairies who dwell within each aspect of nature.

Following this, the practitioner may introduce "symbolic interpretation," a practice that expands on observing nature's signs by interpreting the symbols they encounter with intentional depth. During a walk or meditation, they might notice an animal crossing their path, a particularly striking plant, or an unusual natural formation. In this practice, the practitioner reflects on the qualities of what they observe—perhaps the resilience of a certain flower or the adaptability of a stream bending around rocks—and considers how these traits may hold personal significance. Fairies often reveal symbols that resonate with the practitioner's inner journey, using nature's language to inspire, guide, or provide clarity. This symbolic interpretation becomes a personalized way of receiving the fairies' messages, a process where intuition and connection create a meaningful dialogue between the practitioner and the natural world.

The next step involves "nature's response," a technique for experiencing how nature itself responds to the practitioner's energy. By sitting quietly and extending their awareness outward, they focus on sending a wave of appreciation or gratitude to the surrounding trees, plants, and creatures. They may visualize a gentle, loving energy radiating from their heart, merging with the environment. Often, nature will respond with a subtle change—a rustling of leaves, a gentle breeze, or a bird drawing near. These responses from nature are reflections of the practitioner's openness, amplified by the fairies' presence, who act as conduits of this subtle language. Through this practice, the practitioner realizes that communication with nature is an ongoing exchange, one that reflects both the practitioner's energy and the fairies' guiding influence.

To deepen this exchange, the practitioner learns to engage in "intuitive song and rhythm," a practice that allows them to express appreciation for nature through sound. Sitting in a natural space, they close their eyes and listen to the ambient sounds around them—the rustle of leaves, the trickle of water, the chirping of insects. They then allow a soft, spontaneous sound to arise within themselves, a hum, song, or gentle rhythm, resonating with the sounds they hear. This vocal offering serves as an acknowledgment of the fairies' presence, an expression of unity with nature. Fairies, who are drawn to natural, sincere sounds, often respond by heightening the practitioner's sensitivity or by sending a wave of peaceful energy in return. This practice fosters a playful, sacred connection with nature, as if both the practitioner and the fairies are creating a quiet symphony together.

The practitioner may also incorporate "sacred natural offerings," an act of giving back to the environment as a sign of gratitude. Small, biodegradable offerings—such as flowers, herbs, or natural crystals—are placed near trees, water sources, or areas that feel particularly alive with fairy energy. Each offering is given with gratitude and a silent intention, expressing thanks to the fairies and the spirits of nature for their guidance and companionship. The fairies, ever sensitive to gestures of respect, often leave signs that the offering has been received, perhaps through a gentle breeze or an increase in warmth around the area. This exchange nurtures the bond between the practitioner and the fairies, a quiet promise that acknowledges the interconnectedness of all beings.

Finally, the practitioner explores "dreamtime nature journaling," a technique that opens communication with the fairies and nature through dreams. Before sleep, they hold a simple intention to receive guidance from the natural world and the fairies, placing a natural object—such as a leaf, feather, or small stone—under their pillow or nearby. In the morning, they record any dream images, symbols, or feelings that seem connected to nature. With time, they may notice recurring themes or insights that reflect the fairies' wisdom and guidance. This dreamtime connection offers a way to access messages that may not come through direct observation, revealing layers of meaning that deepen the practitioner's understanding of their relationship with nature.

Through these practices, the practitioner develops a dynamic, living relationship with nature, guided by the fairies' gentle, ever-present energy. Each walk, each meditation, each offering becomes a moment of connection, an invitation to experience life in harmony with the world around. The fairies, guardians of these sacred spaces, impart their wisdom with subtlety, reminding the practitioner that every breath of wind, every ripple of water, and every ray of sunlight speaks of unity and renewal.

In this deepened communication, the practitioner finds that nature is not only a setting but a mentor, a companion, a source of endless wisdom. The fairies, woven into every leaf and stream, every mountain and valley, reveal that life is a conversation, a gentle and sacred exchange that transcends words. As the practitioner continues to listen, to honor, and to respond, they step fully into this partnership with the fairies, walking through the world as a part of its intricate, living harmony, where nature's whispers guide, protect, and inspire each step forward.

Chapter 16
Alignment with Natural Cycles

As the practitioner's connection with the fairies deepens, they begin to attune to the powerful cycles that shape both nature and spirit—the shifting rhythms of the seasons, the phases of the moon, and the ebb and flow of energy that guide the earth's transformations. Fairies, intimately attuned to these natural cycles, act as guides, teaching the practitioner that alignment with these rhythms is more than a spiritual practice; it is a way to harmonize one's inner world with the expansive pulse of nature.

The journey begins with an exploration of the seasonal cycles. Each season holds its unique essence and energy that reflects the life of the earth, and the fairies, bound to these cycles, offer their insights on how to honor each phase. In spring, the earth awakens, and the fairies revel in the budding life and new growth; this is a time for planting intentions, setting goals, and embracing beginnings. The practitioner, guided by the fairies, engages in practices that mirror this energy—planning new projects, refreshing their personal space, and meditating on renewal. Fairies, associated with flowers and sprouting greenery, may reveal themselves through vibrant signs, like the appearance of a specific bloom or a sudden feeling of lightness, reinforcing the spirit of growth.

As the practitioner moves into summer, they align with the season of warmth, vitality, and expansion. Summer is a time when nature is in full bloom, and the fairies celebrate this abundance by dancing through the lush landscapes. The practitioner honors this by embracing their own fullness—nurturing relationships, practicing gratitude, and celebrating the fruits of past intentions. This is also a time for grounding practices, as the intense energy of summer can be both inspiring and overwhelming. Guided by earth fairies, the practitioner may meditate on balance, visualizing their energy as rooted and stable, drawing on the earth's own grounding force to remain centered within the abundance. Fairies often respond to this alignment with summer by intensifying feelings of joy and openness, helping the practitioner feel both expansive and grounded.

In autumn, the energy begins to shift toward release and introspection. The fairies, guardians of this transitional time, celebrate the harvest and the art of letting go, reminding the practitioner that this season holds space for both gratitude and release. To honor autumn, the practitioner reflects on what has served them well and what they are ready to release, embracing the cycle of transformation. They may spend time in nature, feeling the coolness in the air, the change in colors, and the fairies' presence as they guide leaves in their descent. Through rituals of gratitude and cleansing, such as creating a gratitude journal or clearing clutter from their space, the practitioner aligns with the fairies' energy of completion and prepares for the quiet reflection of winter.

Winter, a time of rest and renewal, brings the energy inward, a season that the fairies honor through quietude and stillness. The fairies teach that winter is not a season of absence but a time of deep, quiet renewal, where the earth rests in preparation for new life. During winter, the practitioner embraces solitude, reflection, and introspection, creating space to listen deeply to their own heart. Fairies who dwell in caves, roots, and the silent snows draw near during this season, supporting the practitioner's inner work. Meditative practices, journaling, and honoring moments of silence become gateways to self-discovery, as the practitioner uses this time to realign intentions, releasing what no longer serves and nurturing the quiet sparks of new ideas.

Beyond the seasons, the practitioner learns to attune to the lunar cycle, a rhythm that the fairies recognize as a reflection of subtle energies. The phases of the moon—new, waxing, full, and waning—each hold distinct qualities that the fairies use to guide nature's cycles and the practitioner's journey. During the new moon, the fairies celebrate beginnings, inspiring the practitioner to plant new seeds of intention. This is a time for quiet goal-setting, a ritual that the fairies may encourage through signs of gentle presence—a soft glow or an unexpected stillness, affirming the power of intention in the moon's first light.

As the moon waxes, growing brighter each night, the fairies guide the practitioner toward expansion, courage, and action. The practitioner takes small steps, aligning their actions with the moon's growing light, feeling the fairies' encouragement in subtle bursts of inspiration or motivation. When the full moon arrives, the practitioner connects to the peak of the moon's energy—a time of celebration, illumination, and reflection. The fairies often enhance this energy, encouraging the practitioner to celebrate achievements, express gratitude, or engage in a ritual of self-acceptance. Finally, during the waning moon, the fairies guide the practitioner toward release, allowing energies to calm and return to stillness. This is a time for cleansing, rest, and letting go, a moment where the practitioner aligns with the fairies' own rhythms of retreat and renewal.

To deepen this connection, the practitioner may create a seasonal altar that reflects both the time of year and the lunar phase. Using natural elements—stones, leaves, water, or candles—the practitioner sets up an altar that celebrates the current season's essence and the moon's influence. Each item on the altar serves as a symbol, a tangible connection to the earth's cycles and the fairies' presence within them. Seasonal colors, scents, and textures create a sensory experience that mirrors the fairies' reverence for nature's cycles, reminding the practitioner of their own place within this rhythm.

A final practice, moonlit meditation, draws on the lunar cycle as a powerful tool for reflection and alignment. On a night when the moon is visible, the practitioner sits quietly in its light, opening themselves to the fairies' guidance and feeling the presence of the moon's energy as it bathes them. With each breath, they align with the phase of the moon—focusing on beginnings, growth, celebration, or release as appropriate. Fairies, naturally attuned to the moon's phases, often enhance this experience by creating a heightened sense of peace, a reminder that alignment with the moon's rhythm is a way of honoring life's constant flow. This moonlit meditation becomes a sacred time, a moment where the practitioner feels connected not only to nature but to the fairies who walk with them through each cycle.

Through these practices, the practitioner learns that alignment with natural cycles is an act of harmony, a way to live in rhythm with both nature and spirit. Each season, each phase of the moon, becomes an opportunity to learn, to grow, and to let go, guided by the fairies who embody the wisdom of these cycles. In embracing this rhythm, the practitioner discovers a profound peace, an understanding that just as nature flows through cycles of renewal, so too does the spirit.

The fairies, guardians of this sacred balance, walk alongside, their presence a reminder that life is not static but a journey of transformation, a dance through light and shadow, growth and rest. As the practitioner steps into this flow, they find that each cycle is a gift, a moment to honor both the natural world and their own inner landscape, forever entwined in the harmony of the earth's gentle, unceasing rhythm.

A significant aspect of this deepened alignment involves personalized seasonal rituals—practices that allow the practitioner to connect their intentions with the energy of the current season. Beginning in spring, the practitioner performs a ritual of new beginnings, symbolically planting seeds that represent hopes, dreams, or projects they wish to grow. Guided by the fairies, they may scatter wildflower seeds or plant herbs, each one a living intention. As these seeds grow, the fairies' presence is felt in the emerging life, reinforcing the practitioner's commitment to nurturing their dreams alongside the rhythms of nature.

In summer, when energy reaches its peak, the practitioner is encouraged to create a ritual of gratitude and abundance, where they express appreciation for both personal growth and the blessings of the earth. Gathering flowers or fruits from nature, they create a small offering, which is placed outdoors as a sign of gratitude to the fairies. This gesture, simple yet meaningful, aligns with the fairies' own sense of abundance, their joy reflected in the fullness of summer's bounty. The fairies often respond with subtle affirmations—a gentle breeze, the sudden appearance of butterflies, or a warm sensation—as if blessing the offering and honoring the practitioner's recognition of life's gifts.

Autumn invites the practitioner to partake in rituals of release, a time to reflect on what has been fulfilled and to let go of what no longer serves. Inspired by the falling leaves, the practitioner writes down anything they wish to release—old fears, habits, or thoughts—on small pieces of paper, which are then respectfully burned or buried. The fairies, whose wisdom is tied to nature's cycles of death and rebirth, stand by as silent witnesses, offering a sense of peace and closure. The ritual transforms this release into an act of cleansing, making space for new growth. Through the fairies' guidance, the practitioner learns to see release as a natural part of life's journey, a way of honoring the past while embracing the future.

With the arrival of winter, the practitioner creates a ritual of rest and renewal, aligning with the fairies who retreat to quiet, protected places during this time. They may light a candle, sit quietly in reflection, and focus on inner renewal, setting intentions for the inner work they wish to pursue. Winter's silence becomes a mirror for their own inner stillness, where new inspirations and insights quietly take shape, nurtured by the fairies' unseen presence. The fairies, who understand the strength found in rest, inspire the practitioner to honor this phase without rush or expectation, knowing that winter's quietude is necessary for spring's coming vitality.

Beyond seasonal cycles, the practitioner now learns to synchronize their rituals with the phases of the moon, each phase offering a unique energy that enhances specific intentions. During the new moon, the fairies encourage the practitioner to focus on setting intentions, planting the seeds of ideas and aspirations. A simple new moon ritual might involve sitting beneath the night sky, holding a crystal, flower, or symbol of the practitioner's goal, and speaking intentions quietly to the fairies. This moment of planting is honored as sacred, the new moon's darkness mirroring the mystery and potential of new beginnings.

As the moon waxes, or grows in light, the practitioner engages in rituals of manifestation and growth. Guided by the fairies, they take steps to bring their intentions closer to reality, perhaps through visualizations or small, tangible actions. Each day of the waxing moon becomes a period of nurturing these dreams, with the fairies' encouragement felt as bursts of motivation or subtle signs of progress. The practitioner learns to view this phase as an ongoing collaboration, where both their own efforts and the fairies' guidance work in harmony to cultivate growth.

At the full moon, the practitioner celebrates the culmination of their efforts. The fairies, drawn to the full moon's energy, often amplify this phase's powerful qualities, encouraging rituals of gratitude, clarity, and illumination. The practitioner might hold a personal celebration, lighting candles or placing flowers around a sacred space, reflecting on what has been achieved, and thanking both themselves and the fairies for their support. This ritual of fullness becomes a reminder that their efforts, combined with the fairies' unseen influence, have brought about transformation and achievement.

With the moon's gradual waning, the practitioner shifts focus to release and reflection. Just as the moon's light decreases, so too does the need for outward activity; instead, the practitioner turns inward, releasing what has been completed and reflecting on any lessons learned. Guided by the fairies, they perform simple rituals of cleansing—perhaps using water or smudging with herbs—to clear any stagnant energy. The fairies, who move gracefully with the cycles of change, inspire the practitioner to let go with ease, trusting that release is a natural and necessary part of the journey. This practice closes the lunar cycle, preparing the practitioner to begin again with the next new moon.

To integrate these cycles further, the practitioner is introduced to the practice of seasonal journaling—a method of recording reflections, intentions, and personal insights through each phase of the year and the moon. The journal becomes a place to capture not only personal thoughts but the fairies' messages, symbols, or signs noticed along the way. Over time, patterns emerge, and the practitioner begins to see how each season, each lunar phase, has shaped their growth and deepened their connection with the fairies. This journal becomes a treasured guide, a record of cycles and rhythms that reflects their evolving journey.

In the final practice, ritual alignment with the solstices and equinoxes, the practitioner learns to honor the key turning points of the year as profound spiritual thresholds. During the winter and summer solstices, and the spring and autumn equinoxes, the practitioner performs rituals that mark these transitions, aligning with the fairies who celebrate the earth's great rhythms. At each solstice, they might create an altar with symbols of light and dark, reflecting the year's longest and shortest days, or gather flowers, stones, and leaves during equinoxes to honor balance. The fairies, guardians of these cosmic thresholds, guide the practitioner through these sacred celebrations, deepening their understanding of life's perpetual dance between growth and rest, light and shadow.

Through these advanced practices, the practitioner discovers that aligning with natural cycles is a way of living in harmony with all that is. Each season, each lunar phase, becomes a reminder of life's fluidity, where growth and stillness, beginning and end, are woven into a seamless rhythm. The fairies, whose presence graces every moment of this journey, remind the practitioner that life itself is a series of cycles, each one leading to deeper understanding, peace, and connection with the world.

As the practitioner walks in tune with these rhythms, they embody a timeless wisdom, a quiet strength that comes from recognizing and honoring the cycles of both nature and spirit. The fairies, who whisper softly through each phase, remain close, gentle guides on this path of alignment and harmony. In this way, the practitioner's journey becomes a reflection of the earth's own rhythms—a life in balance, rich with meaning, nurtured by the fairies' unseen, ever-present hand.

Chapter 17
Practices for the Community

As the practitioner's journey with fairies deepens, they begin to see that the magic of these beings extends beyond personal practice, offering ways to enrich and harmonize entire communities. Fairies, whose presence permeates forests, rivers, and gardens, are not bound by solitude; they are caretakers of collective spaces, nurturing balance and vitality in the natural world and in human gatherings.

The foundation of community practices with fairies begins with intentional gatherings—spaces where individuals gather with open hearts, unified by a purpose that resonates with the fairy realm's ideals of respect, kindness, and joy. In preparation for such gatherings, the practitioner creates a welcoming environment infused with symbols and elements from nature. Fresh flowers, herbs, crystals, and representations of the four elements are placed intentionally to honor the fairies and to invite them to be part of the gathering. These elements act as silent invitations, signaling to the fairies that this is a gathering aligned with the earth's harmony.

The first communal ritual introduced is the Circle of Peace, a gathering where participants join hands in a symbolic circle, each person grounding their energy and focusing on creating a peaceful, harmonious space. The practitioner, acting as a guide, encourages participants to close their eyes, breathe deeply, and visualize the energy of peace expanding outward, filling the circle and extending into the surrounding environment. In this quiet space, the fairies' presence may be felt through a gentle breeze, a sudden stillness, or even the subtle appearance of natural symbols, like leaves falling softly or birds drawing near.

This circle strengthens bonds within the group and creates an atmosphere of calm and unity, a reflection of the fairies' own balanced nature.

Another transformative practice is the Community Altar of Intentions, where each participant is invited to bring a small, natural object that symbolizes a personal or collective intention—such as healing, prosperity, or protection. The practitioner arranges these objects on a shared altar, creating a focal point for the group's collective intentions. As the altar grows with offerings, the fairies' energy amplifies, enriching the intentions with the blessings of nature. At the end of the gathering, each person is invited to take a moment at the altar, silently thanking the fairies for their support and sensing the altar's vibrant energy. This shared altar becomes a sacred space that holds the group's collective hopes and dreams, a reminder that individual energies can combine to create powerful, unified change.

The practitioner also introduces the Ritual of Shared Healing, a ceremony where each participant is encouraged to visualize healing energy flowing through the group, guided by the fairies' nurturing presence. During this ritual, participants form a close circle, each person placing a hand on their neighbor's shoulder or holding hands, creating a chain of energy. The practitioner then guides the group through a visualization, where each person envisions soft, radiant light flowing from one person to the next, weaving through the group like threads of a shared tapestry. The fairies, drawn to this circle of unity, often enhance the healing energy, providing a deep sense of peace and renewal. This ritual reminds each participant of the interconnectedness of all beings, a bond that fairies cherish and protect.

Another profound practice is the Seasonal Celebration Ceremony, where the group gathers to honor the turning of the seasons in a community setting. Each participant brings symbols of the current season—flowers in spring, fallen leaves in autumn, water collected from a river in summer, or stones and branches during winter. Together, these offerings are placed in the center of the gathering space, creating a seasonal altar that celebrates the earth's cycles. The practitioner guides the group through a meditation that connects each person with the energy of the season, fostering a collective alignment with nature's rhythms. The fairies, who live in harmony with these cycles, often make their presence known, enhancing the celebration with an atmosphere of gentle, grounding energy. These seasonal gatherings strengthen the community's bond with the natural world and with one another, nurturing a shared sense of belonging to the earth.

To deepen the connection, the practitioner introduces Collective Nature Walks, where the group explores a natural space with the intention of observing, listening, and learning from the environment. These walks encourage participants to move mindfully, noticing signs of fairy presence—glowing reflections on leaves, a sudden quieting of sound, or small symbols like feathers or stones that seem to appear in their path. Each participant is encouraged to carry a small journal or sketchbook to capture their impressions and any messages they feel the fairies are offering to the group. The shared experience of walking through nature with awareness creates a space of harmony and reflection, allowing the group to feel the unity that exists between humans and the fairy realm.

In the final practice, the Ceremony of Gratitude for the Land, the group gathers to honor the earth and express gratitude for its endless gifts. This ritual takes place in a natural setting, where each participant offers something to the land—a handful of seeds, a small stone, or even a few drops of water. The practitioner leads the group in a prayer of gratitude, a quiet acknowledgment of the earth's beauty and resilience. The fairies, who serve as guardians of the land, often respond to this gratitude, filling the air with a sense of peace and appreciation. This ceremony strengthens the bond between the community and the natural world, a reminder that true connection begins with respect and thanks.

Through these practices, the practitioner and the group come to understand that the fairies' influence extends beyond the individual, reaching into the collective energy that binds communities together. These gatherings become spaces of healing, reflection, and joy, echoing the fairies' own reverence for the interconnectedness of all life. In honoring both the natural world and one another, the participants create a web of positive energy that nourishes the earth, the fairies, and the community itself.

By bringing these community practices to life, the practitioner embodies a bridge between the human world and the fairy realm, creating spaces where the fairies' gentle wisdom can guide and inspire. In each gathering, each ritual, the community feels the touch of the fairies, whose presence amplifies love, healing, and unity. Through this shared journey, the practitioner and their community come to know that the magic of fairies is not only a private experience but a gift that flows outward, enriching all who are open to the beauty of life's shared connection.

As community practices with the fairies evolve, the practitioner learns to foster deeper harmony, trust, and cohesion among participants. This advanced understanding of community rituals emphasizes the power of collective intention and unity, as the fairies play a unique role in strengthening the bonds that connect people. Through these expanded practices, the practitioner guides their community into an even closer alignment with the energies of the earth and the fairies, allowing each person to experience the subtle magic that flows when a group is united in purpose and reverence.

A foundational practice for deepening community connections is the Gathering of Shared Intentions. In this ceremony, participants are invited to bring an intention that resonates with the group's collective purpose, such as peace, healing, or protection. To amplify the sense of unity, the practitioner prepares a central altar filled with representations of each intention: feathers for freedom, candles for hope, and stones for stability. Each participant is given a small token, such as a pebble or a flower petal, upon which they can silently focus their intention. As each person adds their token to the altar, a palpable sense of collective energy fills the space. The fairies, drawn to the focused intention of the group, often enhance this energy, creating a subtle feeling of warmth or clarity that permeates the gathering.

In alignment with this practice, the group may participate in a Ceremony of Harmony and Grounding. This ritual serves to synchronize the energies of each individual, creating a balanced, centered space that the fairies can more easily align with. Gathering in a natural setting, participants form a circle and, led by the practitioner, each places a hand on the earth, drawing on the grounding energy of nature. The fairies, who naturally work with the earth's grounding properties, join in this collective grounding, often enhancing participants' sensations of stability and calm. This practice helps each person feel connected to the earth, to one another, and to the fairy realm, a unified presence rooted in harmony and balance.

An advanced practice that builds on the group's sense of unity is the Elemental Invocation Circle. In this ceremony, participants work with the four primary elements—earth, water, fire, and air—each of which is guided by specific fairies. Dividing into small groups, each group represents one element and brings symbols associated with that element to the circle (such as a stone for earth, a shell for water, a candle for fire, and a feather for air). With a sense of shared reverence, each group takes a turn calling upon their element and its guardian fairies, expressing gratitude and asking for the element's blessing. As each element is invoked, the energies intertwine, creating a powerful, balanced atmosphere. The fairies' presence becomes almost tangible, enhancing the ritual with a sense of unity, as each participant feels both their individuality and their connection to the whole.

To deepen the collective harmony, the practitioner may lead a Shared Breath Ceremony, a practice that unifies the group through synchronized breathing. Standing or sitting in a circle, participants close their eyes and are guided to breathe together, each inhaling and exhaling as one. This shared rhythm of breath becomes a moving meditation, a reminder that all life is interconnected. As the group breathes together, the fairies are naturally drawn to the synchronicity, enhancing the group's focus and calm. The collective breathing gradually becomes slower and more profound, creating a sacred space where each individual feels their connection to the life force that flows through nature, humanity, and the fairy realm. This practice builds trust and a deep sense of peace, anchoring the group in shared presence.

Another advanced community practice is the Circle of Healing Affirmations, where participants create a collective affirmation to bring peace, healing, or transformation to the group or a larger community. The practitioner invites each person to share a word or phrase that reflects an aspect of healing, such as "love," "peace," or "renewal." These words are then woven into a single affirmation, which the group repeats together. The fairies, who are attuned to the healing energies within words and sounds, respond to the vibration of these affirmations, magnifying their impact. This shared affirmation transforms into a wave of healing energy that radiates outward, touching each participant and reaching into the broader community. The group often feels the fairies' energy as a gentle sensation that flows between them, a reminder of the transformative power that emerges from unified voices.

A final, powerful practice is the Nature Mandala Creation, where the group gathers natural objects—leaves, stones, flowers, and branches—to create a mandala on the earth. This mandala symbolizes the unity, diversity, and balance within the group, with each object representing a unique aspect of the collective energy. As participants place each item mindfully within the mandala, they may offer a silent blessing or intention. Once the mandala is complete, the practitioner leads a quiet meditation, allowing the group to contemplate the beauty and harmony they have co-created. The fairies, whose energy is naturally drawn to patterns and sacred geometry, often enhance the experience, leaving subtle signs of their presence, such as glimmers on the leaves or a heightened sense of tranquility. This shared mandala serves as a testament to the unity of the group, a physical reminder that their combined energies create something beautiful and enduring.

These advanced practices not only enhance community bonds but foster a collective energy that reflects the harmony and balance the fairies cherish. Each ritual, ceremony, and gathering becomes a living testament to the power of shared purpose, reminding participants that they are part of something larger, something that transcends the individual. In honoring both their unique spirits and their interconnectedness, the group experiences the gentle yet profound impact of the fairies, whose presence nurtures, supports, and uplifts each soul.

Through these practices, the practitioner and their community build a space of enduring unity and love, a reflection of the fairies' timeless wisdom. These gatherings become more than rituals; they become moments where hearts meet, where hands join, and where the whispers of the fairy realm echo in the shared breath of the community. In this space, each person feels the beauty of belonging, the strength of unity, and the quiet yet powerful presence of the fairies, guardians of the earth's sacred harmony.

Chapter 18
Inner Wisdom Ritual

As the practitioner's journey deepens, they are drawn to the quiet well of inner wisdom, a source of insight and clarity that lies within each soul. The fairies, guardians of subtle truths, guide the practitioner to explore this inner landscape, where intuition and spiritual understanding reside.

The path to inner wisdom begins with Guided Reflection, a practice that creates a sacred space for self-discovery. In preparation, the practitioner gathers symbols of grounding and clarity, such as crystals or specific plants that resonate with their journey. Sitting in a quiet space, they center themselves, inviting the fairies' presence to create an atmosphere of calm. Through gentle visualization, the practitioner imagines themselves walking along a path that leads deep into their own consciousness, guided by the subtle glow of the fairies' energy. As they journey inward, they ask open-ended questions, allowing their intuition to respond with images, words, or feelings. The fairies, ever attuned to the flow of energy, may provide affirmations through subtle signs, such as a sudden sense of warmth or a gentle sensation of peace. This practice reveals that inner wisdom is not distant; it is a voice within, waiting to be heard.

Another essential tool for unlocking inner wisdom is the Mirror of Reflection, a ritual in which the practitioner gazes into a bowl of water or a reflective surface, connecting with their own essence. The fairies, who hold a deep connection to water as a conduit for memory and intuition, enhance this ritual by amplifying the reflective properties of the water. The practitioner gazes into the reflection, breathing deeply and allowing their mind to settle into stillness. As they watch the ripples and reflections, insights begin to emerge, their own subconscious speaking in symbols and images. The fairies, who guide these visions, often provide impressions that deepen the practitioner's understanding, showing that true wisdom flows like water—quiet, clear, and gentle. This ritual becomes a meditation of self-connection, where inner truths are revealed without force, arising naturally from within.

To further engage with inner wisdom, the practitioner learns the Ritual of Whispered Questions, a practice inspired by the fairies' own love of silence and subtlety. In this ritual, the practitioner enters a peaceful outdoor space, surrounded by trees, flowers, or stones. Standing with eyes closed, they pose a question to their inner self, phrasing it as a gentle whisper and allowing the words to dissolve into the air. The fairies, drawn by the quiet reverence of the ritual, respond through nature—a rustle of leaves, the song of a bird, or a sudden breeze. Each sign is a response, a part of the conversation between the practitioner and their inner wisdom. This practice teaches that wisdom often comes through quiet observation, and that the world around reflects the answers already held within.

The practitioner then explores the Path of Silent Meditation, a practice that cultivates stillness as a foundation for receiving insights. Sitting outdoors or in a space filled with natural elements, the practitioner closes their eyes and allows themselves to focus solely on their breath, grounding into the present moment. As they breathe, they imagine their breath as a thread that connects them to the fairies' presence, a bridge between their inner self and the spirit of nature. The fairies, who inhabit these quiet spaces, often bring a subtle shift in perception, enhancing the practitioner's sensitivity to inner thoughts and emotions. Through this quiet, focused meditation, insights arise not as sudden revelations but as gentle understandings, emerging from the depths of the practitioner's own awareness. This practice becomes a way of accessing wisdom not by searching, but by simply being, allowing wisdom to reveal itself naturally.

In the Journal of Dream Messages, the practitioner connects with their subconscious by recording dreams each morning, viewing them as messages from their inner world. The fairies, known to work within the dream realm, are often said to communicate through symbols and impressions during sleep, guiding the practitioner toward deeper self-knowledge. Upon waking, the practitioner records any images, feelings, or narratives that linger, treating each as a symbolic message. Patterns often emerge over time, revealing insights and guiding the practitioner's journey. Through this practice, the fairies help to reveal that wisdom is not confined to waking hours but is woven into the fabric of the subconscious. By honoring dreams as a pathway to inner truth, the practitioner learns that wisdom is always present, gently guiding each step.

Finally, the practitioner engages in the Ritual of Inner Council, a visualization practice where they connect with aspects of their own inner wisdom, symbolized as ancient guides or wise figures. In a calm space, they visualize entering a forest or a garden, where they encounter these guides—perhaps a wise elder, a calm protector, or a joyful child. These figures, extensions of their own inner wisdom, offer guidance, reassurance, and answers to questions posed by the practitioner. The fairies, who delight in the transformation of spirit, enhance this experience, creating a sense of connection that feels both familiar and profound. Each guide speaks to a different part of the practitioner's inner self, reminding them that wisdom is multifaceted and that answers often come from embracing every part of their journey.

Through these rituals and practices, the practitioner builds a relationship with their inner wisdom, learning to listen with the heart as much as with the mind. The fairies, silent allies in this journey, reveal that inner truth is as natural as the cycles of nature, always present and waiting to be uncovered. As the practitioner grows in trust and clarity, they discover that the true purpose of wisdom is not simply to know, but to guide, inspire, and bring balance to the spirit. The fairies' quiet guidance teaches that wisdom is gentle, subtle, and deeply personal—a reflection of both nature's beauty and the practitioner's unique journey.

The journey into inner wisdom begins with the Practice of Symbol Interpretation, where the practitioner learns to read the subtle language of symbols that emerge in meditations, dreams, and nature. The fairies, masters of the symbolic and unseen, lend their presence as the practitioner examines recurring images—such as feathers, water, or light—that appear in their practice. By recording these symbols in a dedicated journal, the practitioner begins to decipher patterns and meanings that speak to their unique path. Guided by intuition and the fairies' subtle influence, each symbol becomes a piece of a larger tapestry, reflecting the practitioner's growth, questions, and insights. Over time, the practitioner realizes that these symbols offer timeless wisdom, like whispered guidance from the fairies, aligned with the truth of their journey.

To deepen this connection, the practitioner engages in the Ritual of the Speaking Stone. This ancient practice involves selecting a small, smooth stone from nature—a token that represents stability, memory, and the quiet endurance of wisdom. Holding the stone in their hand, the practitioner enters a state of meditative reflection, asking a specific question or seeking guidance on a personal matter. In the stillness, they listen for insights that may arise, trusting that the fairies will weave their energy into the response. The stone, infused with the practitioner's intention, becomes a touchstone that they can carry, a grounding reminder of the fairies' guidance. Each time the practitioner holds the stone, they reconnect with the wisdom offered during the ritual, grounding themselves in the quiet assurance of inner knowing.

The practitioner then explores the Mirror Meditation, a practice that combines visualization and self-reflection to reveal hidden layers of inner wisdom. Sitting before a mirror, they light a candle, symbolizing clarity and illumination. Gazing into their own reflection, they imagine the fairies gathering around, their presence softening any barriers between conscious and subconscious thought. This ritual allows the practitioner to observe their own essence, free of judgment or expectation. With the fairies' gentle energy, they begin to perceive not only the surface self but the depths of their spirit, unveiling truths that often remain hidden in daily life. This practice becomes a gentle exercise in self-acceptance, where wisdom arises from a profound sense of compassion for the self.

To strengthen their intuitive response, the practitioner practices the Path of Silent Knowing, a meditation that fosters trust in their first impressions and subtle sensations. Guided by the fairies' sensitivity to energy, they learn to pay attention to the immediate feelings or thoughts that arise when faced with a question or decision. Rather than seeking confirmation externally, the practitioner learns to rely on this initial, instinctive response as an expression of inner wisdom. Over time, this practice teaches them to trust the fairies' influence, sensing that their inner voice aligns with the fairies' guidance, like two currents flowing in harmony. This path becomes a journey of deepening trust, where the practitioner discovers that their inner wisdom, when honored, leads them steadily forward.

In the Ritual of Sacred Writing, the practitioner channels their intuition through the act of journaling, allowing thoughts, reflections, and messages to flow freely onto the page. With the fairies as silent witnesses, they create a space for spontaneous writing, where each word becomes a thread that connects conscious thought with subconscious insight. The practitioner may begin by posing a question or simply opening themselves to any message that wishes to emerge. Writing without pause or censorship, they allow the words to unfold naturally, capturing fleeting insights and gentle truths. The fairies, attuned to the subtle flow of expression, amplify the clarity and depth of the messages that arise. This ritual becomes a practice of self-dialogue, where inner wisdom speaks freely, guided by the fairies' quiet encouragement.

Another transformative practice is the Circle of Inner Guides, a visualization in which the practitioner calls forth symbolic representations of their own wisdom and strength. Seated in a quiet, sacred space, they visualize themselves surrounded by wise figures—perhaps an elder, a compassionate healer, or a spirit animal, each embodying an aspect of their own inner guidance. With the fairies' presence enhancing the visualization, the practitioner receives counsel, insights, or reassurances from each figure. These inner guides act as channels of the practitioner's own wisdom, illuminating different perspectives and approaches. As the fairies strengthen this circle, the practitioner gains a sense of wholeness and support, feeling that each guide is a facet of their own spirit, revealing wisdom from within.

To complete their exploration, the practitioner creates a Symbolic Wisdom Altar, a sacred space filled with objects that resonate with their inner truth and serve as reminders of the insights gained. Each item—a feather, a crystal, a flower, or a piece of wood—represents a different lesson or aspect of their journey. Arranged thoughtfully, these objects form a tapestry of symbols that embody the practitioner's path. The fairies, drawn to the intentionality of this altar, often leave subtle signs of their presence—a sparkle of light, the gentle fall of a petal, or a warm sensation. This altar becomes a physical representation of inner wisdom, a space the practitioner can return to when seeking clarity or connection with their own truth. Through this practice, the fairies remind the practitioner that wisdom is a journey, one that is continually unfolding and expanding.

These advanced practices deepen the practitioner's relationship with their own inner wisdom, unveiling insights that illuminate their path forward. The fairies, who understand the subtleties of spirit and the language of symbols, support this journey with a gentle, guiding presence. As the practitioner moves between reflection, meditation, and visualization, they discover that inner wisdom is not a destination but a way of being—a way of listening, trusting, and honoring the quiet truths that arise from within. Each ritual, each symbol, becomes a portal to understanding, a bridge between the conscious mind and the vast, intuitive depths of the spirit.

Through this journey, the practitioner learns that inner wisdom flows naturally when they are aligned with the fairies' gentle guidance. This connection becomes a lifelong companion, a presence that whispers softly, helping them navigate life with clarity, compassion, and insight. In honoring their own wisdom, the practitioner walks in harmony with the fairies, embracing the subtle magic that resides in each moment, each breath, each gentle reminder of their soul's innate knowledge.

Chapter 19
Caring for the Altar

As the practitioner's connection with the fairy realm deepens, the need for a dedicated, sacred space becomes ever more essential. The altar, a point of focus and reverence, serves as a bridge between the human world and the realm of fairies. It is here that the practitioner can feel the presence of these elemental beings, inviting their energy into a space imbued with intention, gratitude, and respect.

The process of creating an altar begins with Choosing a Sacred Location. The practitioner selects a place where they feel peaceful and close to nature, whether indoors by a window that lets in natural light or outdoors in a quiet corner of the garden. The fairies, naturally drawn to places of tranquility and harmony, are more likely to visit an altar positioned with care and intention. This chosen space becomes a sanctuary, a dedicated area where the practitioner can retreat, reflect, and invite the fairies into their daily life.

Once the location is chosen, the practitioner focuses on Selecting Elemental Symbols that resonate with the fairies and the natural world. Each element—earth, water, fire, and air—has its own unique symbols, and by incorporating these, the practitioner reflects the fairies' connection to the elements. A small stone or crystal may represent earth; a shell or bowl of water embodies water; a candle or flame signifies fire; and feathers or incense embody air. Each item, carefully selected and placed, invites the fairies associated with each element to feel welcome. This balance of symbols serves as an invitation for fairies of every kind, creating a harmonious energy that reflects their world.

The practitioner then adds Personal Touchstones that carry special meaning. These items, such as a favorite flower, a treasured piece of jewelry, or a written blessing, serve as reminders of the practitioner's intentions and unique journey. These personal touches express sincerity and individuality, two qualities that attract the fairies, who respond to authenticity and heartfelt offerings. The altar thus becomes not only a space of fairy connection but also a reflection of the practitioner's spirit, making it a truly unique and sacred space.

The Offering of Fresh Natural Elements is a key practice in altar care. Fairies are naturally drawn to living energy, and fresh flowers, herbs, leaves, or small fruits placed on the altar signal both respect and hospitality. Each offering is a gift of the earth, a reminder of the practitioner's gratitude for the fairies' presence. Replacing these offerings regularly keeps the altar vibrant and alive, a reflection of the ever-renewing energy of nature. The fairies, sensitive to the intention behind these offerings, often respond with a sense of warmth or tranquility, as though acknowledging the effort and care invested in the altar.

To maintain the altar's energetic harmony, the practitioner practices Energetic Cleansing, clearing the space regularly of stagnant or accumulated energy. The fairies, who are naturally drawn to clear and balanced spaces, resonate deeply with a clean, well-maintained altar. A simple cleansing can be performed by burning incense or herbs, such as sage, lavender, or rosemary, allowing the smoke to purify and refresh the altar. This smoke, gently wafted over each object, carries away any heaviness, leaving only a light, receptive energy that welcomes the fairies. The practitioner may also visualize a gentle light encompassing the altar, renewing its energy and reaffirming the space as one of purity and intention.

In the practice of Seasonal Renewal, the practitioner honors the cycles of nature by updating the altar to reflect the changing seasons. Each season brings unique energy—spring's blossoming growth, summer's warmth, autumn's quiet reflection, and winter's stillness. The practitioner decorates the altar with symbols and colors of the current season, aligning with the fairies' natural rhythms. Fresh blossoms in spring, green leaves or sun-kissed stones in summer, fallen leaves in autumn, and evergreen branches or stones in winter can all reflect this seasonal cycle. This act of seasonal renewal invites the fairies to celebrate the cycles of the earth alongside the practitioner, strengthening their bond through shared observance.

The final foundational practice is Daily Gratitude Rituals, where the practitioner spends a few moments each day at the altar, offering silent gratitude to the fairies for their presence and guidance. With a quiet heart, the practitioner expresses appreciation for both the seen and unseen gifts that the fairies bring, such as feelings of peace, clarity, or small signs in nature. The fairies, attuned to the energy of gratitude, often respond with subtle signs—a shift in light, a feeling of warmth, or a moment of stillness. This daily practice of gratitude keeps the altar vibrant and alive, a space where the practitioner and fairies meet in shared reverence and joy.

Through these foundational practices, the altar becomes more than just a collection of objects; it transforms into a living, breathing space where the fairies feel welcome, and where the practitioner can connect to their inner world and to the spirit of nature. Each element, each offering, becomes an expression of the practitioner's commitment to honoring the fairy realm, creating a space filled with the energy of respect, love, and intention.

As the practitioner tends to their altar, they find that this sacred space also nurtures their own spirit, bringing peace, clarity, and a sense of connection. The fairies, guardians of nature's secrets, feel the sincerity of the practitioner's intentions and often leave gentle reminders of their presence—a shimmer of light, a whisper of wind, or an inner sense of calm. This altar, crafted with care and maintained with love, serves as a bridge to the fairy realm, a place of transformation, harmony, and shared understanding. The practitioner, in tending to this space, learns the essence of devotion, discovering that the care they give is reflected back to them, filling their spirit with a quiet, enduring joy.

The journey of deepening altar care begins with the practice of Consecrating the Altar. The practitioner dedicates the altar as a sacred portal to the fairy realm, a ritual of acknowledgment and intention that signals to the fairies that this space is a true haven of connection. To consecrate the altar, the practitioner may choose to invoke the elements and call upon the fairies associated with each one, inviting their blessings and energy to infuse the space. With a small bowl of salt, a feather, a candle flame, and a shell or water, the practitioner moves clockwise around the altar, gently touching each item and reciting a personal blessing. This act of consecration solidifies the altar as a dedicated space, inviting the fairies' protective and guiding presence to dwell within.

Once consecrated, the practitioner may engage in the Art of Personalization, adding items that reflect specific intentions or aspects of their spiritual path. The fairies, who cherish unique expressions of spirit, are drawn to the individuality of a personalized altar. The practitioner might include personal symbols, such as a carved figurine, a handwritten affirmation, or a small object with personal significance. Over time, each item becomes a thread in the tapestry of the altar, embodying a different layer of intention, memory, and gratitude. This personal touch invites a unique relationship with the fairies, one that speaks to the practitioner's journey and growth.

To amplify the altar's energy, the practitioner can incorporate the Practice of Crystal Grids, using crystals to create a network of energy that enhances the altar's resonance with the fairy realm. Crystals like rose quartz, amethyst, and clear quartz are carefully arranged in geometric patterns that draw in positive energy and amplify the space's vibrational frequency. The practitioner might design a grid specific to their current focus—be it healing, protection, or insight—placing the grid at the center of the altar and visualizing it as a beacon of intention that connects to the fairy realm. The fairies, sensitive to the crystals' pure energy, often respond by enhancing the space with a feeling of warmth, clarity, or peaceful presence, a quiet acknowledgment of the practitioner's intention.

In harmony with the natural cycles, the practitioner engages in Lunar and Seasonal Alterations. This practice involves adapting the altar's elements to reflect the phases of the moon and changes in the seasons, aligning it with the rhythms that guide both nature and the fairies. During the new moon, for instance, the practitioner might clear and refresh the altar, adding symbols of renewal and intention setting. During the full moon, they might add symbols of abundance and gratitude, reflecting the culmination of energies. Each season also brings its own influence: fresh flowers and buds in spring, green leaves or bright stones in summer, autumnal leaves and harvest offerings in fall, and evergreen branches in winter. These alterations keep the altar dynamic and alive, creating a rhythm that mirrors the earth's cycles, deepening the fairies' bond with the practitioner as they align their practices with nature's heartbeat.

For times when the practitioner seeks a specific purpose, the Creation of a Focused Intention Space is a powerful method to invite fairy energy for a particular goal or period. This could be for a time of healing, protection, or growth. The practitioner selects objects that resonate with this purpose—such as candles for clarity, herbs for grounding, or charms for protection—and places them at the center of the altar, surrounding them with symbols of the four elements. The practitioner then speaks their intention aloud, offering it to the fairies with the invitation to aid in manifesting the goal. By focusing their energy, the altar becomes a magnet for the fairies' assistance, a space where intention and fairy presence coalesce to bring guidance and support. This focused intention space can be a temporary setup or a long-term addition, depending on the practitioner's journey.

An advanced ritual for maintaining the altar's harmony is Periodic Energetic Realignment, where the practitioner assesses and resets the altar's energy. This involves both clearing and recharging the space, creating a flow of energy that is balanced and receptive. To realign the altar, the practitioner might use sound, such as a bell or singing bowl, to shift stagnant energy, followed by a visualization of light enveloping the altar, refreshing it with renewed vitality. The fairies, who resonate with harmonious energy, are naturally drawn to a realigned altar, often leaving subtle impressions of their presence—a sense of tranquility, or a soft shimmer on an object. This realignment ritual strengthens the altar's power as a space of connection, making it an even clearer channel for the fairies' energy.

The final practice in advanced altar care is the Interpretation of Energetic Responses from the altar. The practitioner learns to recognize the fairies' subtle responses to their care and offerings, whether it's a feeling of warmth, a sudden stillness, or an intuitive sense of the fairies' presence. These responses serve as affirmations, a gentle acknowledgment of the practitioner's efforts and sincerity. By observing these responses, the practitioner hones their sensitivity, understanding that the fairies' energy flows in harmony with their own. This practice of observation deepens the practitioner's intuition, making the altar a place where communication between realms occurs in whispers, sensations, and moments of quiet realization.

Through these advanced practices, the altar becomes a living reflection of the practitioner's journey and devotion, a space that evolves as they grow, adapting to the rhythms of their spirit and the natural world. Each ritual, each adjustment, becomes an act of alignment, a gesture of respect that invites the fairies ever closer. This sacred space, tended with love and mindfulness, serves as a bridge not only to the fairy realm but to the practitioner's own inner world, where each element and object becomes a symbol of unity, harmony, and shared intention.

In this journey of caring for the altar, the practitioner finds that the space becomes a mirror, a place where they see their own growth, challenges, and joys reflected. The fairies, who delight in this ever-evolving relationship, often respond with gentle signs, a quiet affirmation that their presence is near. Through the altar, the practitioner learns the art of devotion and connection, discovering that the love and care they give returns to them manifold, deepening their bond with the fairies and with the natural rhythm of life itself.

Chapter 20
Advanced Spiritual Protection

In the subtle realms where fairies dwell, protection is not merely a shield against harm but a delicate art—a weaving of intentions, energies, and respect for natural forces. As the practitioner advances in their spiritual journey, they come to recognize the need for heightened forms of protection, ones that resonate with the intricacies of their connection to fairies.

The first step in this journey involves Understanding Energy Shields, a practice rooted in awareness and intention. Energy shields function as invisible barriers, designed to repel negative energies while maintaining harmony with the environment. With the assistance of fairies, these shields become more than just static defenses—they are living, breathing extensions of the practitioner's aura, responding to shifts in energy and need. To initiate this process, the practitioner is encouraged to center themselves in a state of calm, visualizing an enveloping light that surrounds and protects them. This light, infused with the intention of peace and safety, becomes a buffer that the fairies can amplify. Calling upon the fairies to imbue this shield with their subtle energy, the practitioner gains a feeling of heightened security and lightness, an affirmation that the fairies' protective forces are at work.

The Elements of Nature as Protective Allies come into play as well, with each element offering a unique form of defense. Earth, with its grounding qualities, can be used to anchor the practitioner's energy, creating a stable base that resists external disruptions. Stones and crystals, especially black tourmaline, obsidian, or hematite, are placed at the corners of one's space, acting as guardians that absorb and neutralize unwanted energies.

Water, symbolizing fluidity and cleansing, aids in dissolving negativity, and a small bowl of water, when blessed and placed on the altar or near the practitioner, serves as a conduit for the fairies to wash away lingering negativity. Fire, with its transformative power, consumes and transmutes negativity; a candle flame, infused with intention and watched over by the fairies, becomes a radiant source of strength. Lastly, Air, representing clarity and freedom, is called upon to blow away illusions or fears, creating a space that feels light, free, and resilient.

A potent protective method that requires focus and reverence is the Invocation of Fairy Guardians. Certain fairies, with their attunement to protective energies, willingly assist when treated with respect and gratitude. To invoke a fairy guardian, the practitioner may choose a quiet space in nature or a dedicated ritual setting. Here, they offer a small gift—a crystal, a flower, or a few drops of natural oil—to signify their request for protection. As they focus on their intention, they call out to the fairies with sincerity, inviting their presence as protectors of their space and spirit. These fairy guardians, often felt as a presence or sensed as a warmth around the practitioner, lend their energy to the protective shield, enhancing its effectiveness. When such fairies agree to offer their guardianship, they often signal their presence through subtle cues—a rustling of leaves, a shift in the air, or a feeling of peaceful strength.

Fairy Sigils and Symbols of Protection are another powerful tool in the practitioner's spiritual arsenal. Sigils—symbols crafted through intent and infused with meaning—act as conduits for fairy energy, amplifying the strength of protection. To create a fairy sigil, the practitioner begins with an intention, carefully choosing words or images that encapsulate their desired protection. These symbols, drawn on parchment or etched onto a small stone, are then placed on the altar or carried with the practitioner. In quiet moments, they focus on the symbol, inviting the fairies to imbue it with their energy. As the practitioner holds this symbol in mind, it becomes a tangible reminder of their connection to the fairy realm, an object alive with protective energy, responsive to their needs and intentions.

At times, the practitioner may feel the need for heightened defense in the face of intense negativity. For such moments, Cleansing Rites with Fairy Guidance provide both relief and resilience. Using sacred herbs like sage, rosemary, or lavender, the practitioner performs a cleansing ritual, wafting the smoke around themselves or their space. With each movement, they invite the fairies to participate in lifting and dispersing any lingering negativity. The fairies, drawn to the purity of the herbs' scent, add their presence to the cleansing, a quiet yet powerful influence that heightens the ritual's effectiveness. As the smoke disperses, so too does any stagnant energy, leaving the practitioner's space light and renewed.

Finally, the Practice of Energetic Grounding plays a crucial role in maintaining protection. Grounding, a simple yet profound practice, ensures that the practitioner remains connected to the earth, reducing vulnerability to external influences. With their feet on bare ground, the practitioner imagines roots extending from their body into the earth's core, drawing stability and strength from below. This grounding process not only stabilizes their energy but also fortifies their connection to the fairies, who resonate deeply with earth's natural rhythms. By grounding regularly, the practitioner remains balanced, less susceptible to draining influences, and more open to receiving fairy support.

Through these practices, the practitioner builds a tapestry of protection, a living framework that evolves as they deepen their bond with the fairies. In learning to weave energy shields, to invoke guardians, and to connect with elemental allies, they not only safeguard themselves but also honor the fairies' gifts. Each protective act is a dance between realms, a testament to the mutual trust that forms the heart of this connection. With these tools, the practitioner stands as both a guardian of their own energy and a steward of the fairy realm's profound, unseen forces.

As the practitioner's relationship with fairies deepens, so too does the nature of protection evolve—moving from simple safeguards to a complex, intuitive shield. Here, protection becomes more than a barrier; it becomes an art form, a constant dialogue between practitioner and fairy allies. This second part delves further into the intricacies of maintaining and reinforcing protective practices, honing the practitioner's sensitivity to spiritual shifts and enhancing their connection to elemental beings.

With a protective foundation in place, the practitioner learns to Reinforce Energy Shields Through Intentional Recharging. Just as a physical structure requires maintenance, an energy shield thrives on renewal. The practitioner can perform this renewal by consciously invoking their intention to strengthen the shield, visualizing a fresh layer of light or elemental energy infusing it with new vitality. The practitioner sits or stands within their space, eyes gently closed, and visualizes the protective boundary around them. As they breathe deeply, they call upon specific elemental fairies: earth fairies to add grounded strength, fire fairies to imbue transformative resilience, air fairies for mental clarity, and water fairies to bring adaptability. This visualization reinvigorates the shield, allowing it to remain strong, flexible, and responsive to subtle changes.

In moments of heightened need, The Art of Layered Shielding becomes invaluable. Layered shielding consists of creating multiple protective layers, each infused with distinct energies or intentions, and each one progressively refining the shield's purpose. The practitioner begins by creating an initial shield close to their body, visualized as a barrier of light representing calm and neutrality. Next, they add another layer infused with elemental strength, perhaps with the earthy presence of stones or the warmth of a gentle flame. The final layer serves as a filter, connected to fairy energies, that can transmute or dissolve any unwanted forces. This technique of layered protection creates a multidimensional shield that does more than repel energy; it filters, transmutes, and refines the energies entering the practitioner's space, maintaining an unbroken connection to the supportive realm of fairies.

Fairy Tokens for Protective Reinforcement also hold a significant role in advanced spiritual safeguarding. These tokens can be natural objects like stones, leaves, or flower petals—simple items charged with fairy energy to carry on the protective influence. To create a token, the practitioner places their chosen item on a prepared altar, surrounding it with items that represent the four elements. In a quiet moment, they ask the fairies to imbue this token with lasting protection, giving thanks and expressing intention. The fairy energy within the token is then sealed, allowing it to serve as a portable guardian. Carried on one's person, placed at doorways, or kept near the bedside, these tokens act as subtle yet powerful protectors, continuously charged with fairy energy.

Building upon tokens, the practitioner may explore Protective Grids within their space. A protective grid consists of a layout of fairy-blessed stones, crystals, or natural objects arranged in geometric patterns. The practitioner chooses the layout—perhaps a circle for unity, a triangle for focus, or a spiral for growth—and places their charged tokens at points within this pattern. Each object is blessed to work in unison, connecting with the fairy realm to create an ambient field of protection. This grid, left intact within the ritual space or home, establishes a harmonic resonance, warding off disruptive energies while allowing beneficial forces to enter. The fairies, recognizing the intention of such a setup, often join in to enhance its vibrational integrity, fortifying the space in ways both visible and unseen.

Another vital aspect of advanced protection is Sensitivity to Shifts in Energies and Intentional Responses. Over time, the practitioner learns to recognize when energy in their space begins to feel "off" or diminished. These signs might be a sense of heaviness, disturbances in emotional balance, or feelings of unease. When such signals appear, the practitioner calls upon fairies for insight, often receiving guidance through subtle cues or sensations. They then perform a cleansing, releasing any collected energy with gratitude and inviting the fairies to assist in renewing the space. This act of responding to shifts as they arise deepens the practitioner's intuitive bond with the fairies, fostering a relationship based on mutual awareness and care.

In deepening protection further, the practitioner engages in Continuous Rituals of Renewal. As the seasons shift and the moon waxes and wanes, so too do the energy dynamics in one's life and space. By observing these cycles, the practitioner aligns with the ebb and flow of natural energy, using it to amplify protective intentions. At the full moon, for instance, they might invite water fairies to enhance their shield's adaptability, or during a solstice, call on fire fairies to fortify resilience. These rituals of renewal allow for protection that grows with the practitioner, resonating with their inner cycles and the changing rhythms of nature itself.

Finally, Trusting the Bond with Fairy Allies becomes a source of unwavering strength. This trust is built gradually, through a quiet understanding that the fairies respond not only to rituals and offerings but also to the sincerity of the practitioner's heart. It is through this bond that the practitioner finds comfort and courage, recognizing the fairies as steadfast allies who, though unseen, guard and nurture. In moments of vulnerability, they turn inward, sensing the fairies' presence in subtle signs—a breeze, the glimmer of light through leaves, the warmth of the earth beneath. This quiet communion becomes the greatest form of protection, an intangible yet profound shield that nothing can diminish.

Through the wisdom and tools of advanced spiritual protection, the practitioner reaches a new harmony in the balance of strength and sensitivity. With each technique, they refine their intuitive abilities, crafting protection not only as a safeguard but as an act of reverence and connection to the fairies. And thus, the protective journey grows into something sacred—a living testament to the unity between human and fairy, earth and spirit, shadow and light.

Chapter 21
Self-Knowledge and Growth

In the unfolding journey with fairies, the path to self-knowledge marks a profound transition. Here, the practitioner is invited to go beyond understanding the world around them and turn inward, to explore the intricate layers of their own being. Guided by the fairies, this path of self-discovery reveals an internal landscape often hidden or forgotten, a landscape where intuition, memories, emotions, and inner strengths all converge. With each step taken into this realm, the practitioner uncovers truths about themselves that become both guides and mirrors in their spiritual journey.

Fairies, with their ancient wisdom and innate connection to nature, become subtle but insightful companions in this quest. They help the practitioner attune to subtler aspects of their consciousness, to examine not only the emotions on the surface but the undercurrents that shape their thoughts, dreams, and fears. Through this process, self-knowledge emerges not as an abstract idea but as an intimate experience, a connection with the authentic self.

One of the fundamental practices here is Mindful Reflection, a practice enhanced through fairy guidance. In moments of quiet introspection, the practitioner may sit near an open window or within a natural setting, allowing the gentle energies of nature to encourage reflection. With the fairies' energy as a calming presence, the practitioner begins by observing their recent emotions and thoughts, acknowledging them without judgment. This practice of awareness, conducted with a sense of curiosity rather than criticism, helps to illuminate patterns and reactions that may have previously gone unnoticed.

In this presence of fairy energy, the practitioner learns to sit with their own thoughts in acceptance, recognizing each one as a message or a layer of self awaiting understanding.

As this process deepens, the practitioner may engage in Journaling with Fairy Insight. Here, they write down reflections, emotions, dreams, or any recurring thoughts that arise during their time in nature or meditation. Fairies, being intuitive creatures, often communicate in subtle ways—through sensations, images, or symbols that emerge during journaling. The practitioner may notice recurring themes or symbols that hold particular resonance. By recording these insights and returning to them periodically, the practitioner starts to identify areas of growth or healing. This journaling, imbued with fairy wisdom, becomes a personal map, guiding the practitioner back to their inner self with each entry.

Another vital practice in the journey of self-knowledge is Embracing Emotions Through Fairy-Empowered Meditation. When deeply attuned to fairy energy, the practitioner can access an enhanced state of meditation where they not only observe their emotions but also feel supported in releasing or transforming them. This process involves sitting in a sacred space, perhaps near an altar or a chosen natural object, and calling upon the fairies to guide them through their emotional landscape. As emotions surface—whether joy, sadness, fear, or uncertainty—the practitioner allows themselves to feel each fully, trusting the fairies' presence to provide balance and understanding. In this state, emotions are acknowledged as teachers, rather than obstacles, and through them, the practitioner's heart opens further to the fairy realm and to themselves.

Listening to the Body's Signals also becomes a practice in self-discovery. Often, physical sensations or tensions carry unspoken messages that, when addressed, lead to greater self-awareness. Fairies, known for their connection to the natural flow of energy, encourage the practitioner to notice the subtle sensations within their body. Is there a heaviness around the heart, a tightness in the chest, or a tension in the shoulders? In moments of awareness, the practitioner can place their hand on these areas and ask the fairies to help them understand what these sensations represent. Through this practice, the body's signals become not only indicators of physical health but also reflections of the inner self, helping the practitioner to harmonize body, mind, and spirit.

An essential aspect of self-knowledge is Exploring Personal Intentions and Desires with Fairy Guidance. Intentions are the silent currents that shape the practitioner's actions, beliefs, and relationships. With fairy support, the practitioner can delve into their deeper motivations, examining what truly drives them in life. This process may involve setting aside time each day or week to reflect upon a question such as: "What do I genuinely desire?" or "What intention guides my path?" By framing these questions within the context of fairy wisdom, the answers often reveal hidden truths or deeper longings. Through this exploration, the practitioner learns to align their life choices with their authentic self, a self brought to light through fairy guidance.

Through the fairies, the practitioner may also access Inner Child Work, a gentle yet transformative practice of reconnecting with the childlike aspects within themselves. Fairies, with their playful and nurturing energy, are natural allies in helping the practitioner revisit memories of joy, wonder, and innocence that may have been overshadowed by adulthood's burdens. In quiet moments, the practitioner can invite the fairies to guide them to memories or experiences where they felt connected to their truest self. As these memories surface, the practitioner may relive them, feeling the emotions, smells, sounds, and sensations as if they were happening anew. Through this practice, they reawaken the inner child's joy and curiosity, integrating these qualities into their present life, cultivating a more fulfilled and vibrant sense of self.

Recognizing Shadows with Fairy Support becomes another pivotal part of self-discovery. Fairies, while often gentle and light-hearted, also possess a natural understanding of life's dualities. They help the practitioner to face and embrace their own shadows—those aspects of the self that are hidden or denied. With their presence, the practitioner learns to approach these aspects not with fear but with openness, understanding that the shadow holds valuable wisdom. By working with fairies to confront and integrate these parts of themselves, the practitioner transforms resistance into acceptance, and avoidance into healing.

In the pursuit of self-knowledge, Expressing Gratitude to Fairies for Personal Growth becomes an anchor, grounding each discovery in appreciation. Through gratitude rituals, the practitioner thanks the fairies for their guidance, whether through a simple offering of flowers, a few whispered words, or the lighting of a candle. This gratitude strengthens the connection, reaffirming that the journey of self-discovery is one shared between realms. In acknowledging the fairies' role, the practitioner understands that their growth is supported, that they are not alone on this path to self-awareness.

In every aspect of self-knowledge explored with fairies, the practitioner steps closer to an inner truth that is simultaneously personal and universal. With the fairies' presence, self-knowledge becomes a journey not just into one's own depths but into a realm of collective wisdom shared between human and fairy, earth and spirit. Each discovery, each insight, brings the practitioner to a greater harmony with themselves and with the mysteries of the world they inhabit. The journey of self-knowledge, enriched by the fairies' gentle wisdom, opens doors that lead not only inward but beyond, into a connectedness with all life.

Having begun the path of self-knowledge with the fairies' guidance, the practitioner now moves deeper, unearthing layers of inner understanding and personal growth. At this stage, the connection with the fairies matures, and they reveal subtler dimensions of self-awareness. This is not merely an expansion of what has been discovered but a journey into integrating self-knowledge into everyday life, allowing personal growth to become a living, breathing process woven into each action, thought, and interaction.

Central to this deepening journey is Self-Assessment with Fairy Reflection. The fairies, with their gentle wisdom, assist the practitioner in regularly evaluating their own growth, reflecting on changes in behavior, responses, and intentions. This self-assessment practice can take place at the end of each day or week, where the practitioner asks themselves, "What insights have I gained?" or "How have I acted in alignment with my true self?" Through fairy guidance, these reflections reveal the delicate progress the practitioner makes, even in small moments. Fairies, being sensitive to intention, encourage honesty and self-compassion, reminding the practitioner that self-awareness grows slowly, like roots deepening into the earth.

As the practitioner continues, they encounter moments where emotions, habits, or responses remain unclear or tangled. Embracing Self-Compassion through Fairy Affirmations becomes a pivotal practice. Fairies, who naturally radiate acceptance and understanding, guide the practitioner to speak to themselves with kindness, especially during times of self-doubt or internal conflict. The practitioner may create affirmations inspired by fairy energy, phrases like "I am growing with patience" or "I trust in my journey," whispered during meditation or written in a journal. By regularly affirming themselves in this way, the practitioner begins to see their self-growth as a nurturing process, honoring each step as part of a larger journey.

In moments of difficulty or shadow, the fairies introduce The Practice of Mirror Reflection with Fairy Presence. This exercise invites the practitioner to sit quietly with a mirror, gazing softly at their own reflection, while holding an image or symbol of fairy energy nearby, such as a crystal, feather, or small flower. In the mirror's reflection, the practitioner sees not only their face but their emotions and thoughts as if mirrored back with fairy wisdom. Fairies offer their gentle guidance here, encouraging the practitioner to observe their own eyes, to notice expressions of emotion, and to accept these aspects of themselves without judgment. Through this, the practitioner experiences self-acceptance, witnessing both their strengths and vulnerabilities in a compassionate light.

To deepen their journey, the practitioner may engage in Visualization of Life's Path Guided by Fairies. In this visualization, the practitioner imagines walking along a forest path, guided by fairies who appear in various forms—perhaps as gentle lights or whispering leaves. As the practitioner walks, they visualize significant moments of their past that emerge along the path, moments of joy, challenge, learning, and transformation. The fairies, with their natural wisdom, help the practitioner to acknowledge and integrate these memories, understanding that each moment contributes to their present self. This visualization becomes a way to honor life's journey and recognize that growth, supported by the fairies, is both continuous and evolving.

Fairies also introduce Creative Expression as a Gateway to Inner Wisdom, a practice of engaging with creativity to unlock hidden insights. The practitioner may feel drawn to paint, write poetry, dance, or create music inspired by their journey with fairies. This act of creation becomes a bridge to the subconscious, where inner truths often reside. As the fairies inspire colors, shapes, or words, the practitioner finds that creativity becomes an intuitive tool, revealing emotions and insights that words alone cannot capture. Through this creative expression, they access a form of self-knowledge that is felt rather than analyzed, resonating deeply within the heart.

The practice of Cultivating Silence and Inner Listening also becomes essential at this stage. Fairies, who dwell in quiet, hidden places, remind the practitioner of the power found in moments of stillness. In a simple act of sitting in silence—perhaps under a tree or by a window open to the night—the practitioner listens not for voices but for the subtle stirrings within their own mind and spirit. These moments of silence allow deeper realizations to surface without force, gently guiding the practitioner toward self-truths that arise naturally, just as a leaf floats to the forest floor. In these quiet moments, the fairies' presence is sensed as a warm, supportive energy that allows the practitioner to explore their own depths with patience.

As self-knowledge deepens, the fairies encourage A Ritual of Personal Commitment to Growth. This ritual need not be elaborate; it may involve lighting a single candle or holding a small token that represents personal growth, such as a stone or feather. In this ritual, the practitioner silently or aloud states their commitment to continue their journey of self-knowledge, acknowledging both the fairies' guidance and their own inner strength. By making this vow, the practitioner reaffirms their intention to live authentically, to grow continually, and to embrace each aspect of themselves with courage. This commitment becomes an energetic anchor, a point of return whenever challenges arise on the path.

In this stage, Mindful Interaction with Others as a Mirror of Inner Growth is introduced. Fairies, who understand the interconnectedness of all beings, guide the practitioner to view interactions with others as reflections of their own growth. Each interaction—whether peaceful or challenging—becomes an opportunity for self-reflection, a chance to observe one's reactions, words, and emotions in real-time. Fairies remind the practitioner that relationships mirror inner growth, showing not only how they perceive others but also how they perceive themselves. Through this, the practitioner learns patience, compassion, and understanding, recognizing that every connection is part of the intricate web of their spiritual path.

With this deepened self-knowledge, the practitioner finds themselves more aligned with their true nature and better equipped to navigate life with clarity and purpose. The fairies, silent yet present, become enduring companions, their wisdom gently woven into the fabric of each moment. As the practitioner looks forward, they know that self-knowledge is not an end but a foundation—a ground upon which the next steps of their spiritual path will be built, always growing, always evolving.

Chapter 22
Manifestation Practices

In the heart of creation lies a powerful truth: every thought, every feeling, and every intention shapes reality. As we step into the realm of manifestation, we engage in an ancient dance with the energies that form our world. Manifestation practices invite us to consciously direct this energy, drawing upon the fairy realm as guides and collaborators. The fairies, attuned to the natural flow of life, gently teach the practitioner how to set intentions and harness their inner will to bring desires into form. This is not mere wishful thinking; it is a profound, deliberate alignment with the universe's creative force.

At the core of manifestation lies Clarity of Intention. Fairies, who move with precision and purpose through the elements, encourage the practitioner to refine their desires with crystal-clear focus. Before beginning any practice, the practitioner is guided to sit quietly and meditate on the essence of their desire. What is the heart of this wish? Does it arise from a place of true need or from fleeting desire? By understanding the roots of their intentions, they align with deeper values, and fairies assist in grounding these intentions, lending them a subtle yet powerful foundation that feels deeply aligned with nature's flow.

The next step is Creating an Intention Statement. Here, the practitioner distills their desire into a single, potent phrase, spoken as if the outcome is already a reality. An intention for prosperity, for instance, might become, "I am surrounded by abundance and prosperity, flowing effortlessly into my life." Fairies, whose energy is direct and unburdened by hesitation, encourage the practitioner to speak this statement aloud with conviction. In doing so, the words become more than mere language; they transform into a seed of energy, ready to grow in the fertile field of possibility.

To reinforce this intention, the practitioner is introduced to The Use of Symbols and Fairy Elements. Fairies have long associated themselves with specific plants, stones, and symbols that resonate with various aspects of life. In the manifestation process, the practitioner might select a crystal, leaf, or flower that corresponds to their desire—citrine for prosperity, lavender for calm, or rose petals for love. This chosen item becomes a tangible anchor for the intention, carrying the vibration of both the desired outcome and the fairy energy that enhances it. By keeping this item close, the practitioner nurtures a constant, subtle connection to their desire, as if whispering to it through the energies of nature.

Visualization, a powerful technique of manifestation, comes next. Guided by Fairy Imagination, the practitioner is encouraged to close their eyes and visualize their intention as though it is unfolding in the present moment. Fairies, beings of rich imagination and creativity, guide the practitioner to see every detail vividly, feel the emotions tied to the desired outcome, and truly live in this vision. If the intention is for peace, the practitioner may imagine themselves surrounded by a serene forest, feeling the quiet calm of fairy energy around them. This visualization creates a sensory experience so vivid that the desire feels real and immediate, allowing it to magnetically draw corresponding energies toward the practitioner.

Another essential practice is Grounding the Intention with Elemental Energy. In nature, fairies channel their energy through the four elements—earth, water, fire, and air. Here, they teach the practitioner how to integrate these elemental forces to support manifestation. For grounding and stability, the practitioner may connect to earth energy, perhaps by placing their hands on soil or holding a stone. For adaptability and flow, they might work with water by meditating near a stream or including a small bowl of water in their ritual. Fire, ignited through a candle, fuels passion and transformation, while air, symbolized by incense or a gentle breeze, carries the intention outward. This elemental grounding roots the intention in the natural world, aligning it with the rhythms of life.

Fairies also teach the Practice of Release and Trust, an often overlooked yet crucial part of manifestation. After setting their intention and grounding it, the practitioner must release their desire to the universe with trust, allowing it to manifest in its own time. Fairies, who move effortlessly within the cycles of nature, remind the practitioner that growth, too, has its seasons. Just as a flower blooms when it is ready, so will their desire come into being when conditions are right. Through this release, the practitioner frees themselves from attachment, trusting in the natural flow and timing, confident that the fairies continue to support the journey.

In moments of uncertainty, the fairies introduce Signs and Symbols of Affirmation. As the practitioner moves through daily life, they remain open to subtle messages from the fairies and nature itself. A butterfly landing nearby, a sudden breeze, or an unexpected encounter with a meaningful symbol—all become affirmations that the intention is moving toward realization. These signs, often subtle yet unmistakable, act as reminders that the fairies are guiding and

As the journey of manifestation deepens, so too does the connection between practitioner and the delicate energies of the fairy realm. In this stage, the fairies guide the practitioner into more refined techniques, encouraging practices that both strengthen intention and amplify the energy around it. Here, we encounter the art of Energetic Alignment and Daily Integration, cultivating a life that resonates harmoniously with the desired manifestation.

The first step is Harmonizing Intentions with Daily Actions. Fairies, who embody harmony with nature, reveal the importance of consistency between intention and action. Manifestation, they teach, is not limited to moments of ritual or focused intention but flourishes in the rhythm of everyday life. For instance, if the practitioner seeks peace, they are encouraged to adopt practices that embody calmness—gentle conversations, reflective moments, and interactions that nurture tranquility. By living in alignment with their intentions, they become a channel for the energies they wish to manifest, allowing them to take form naturally.

To enhance this daily alignment, fairies introduce the Practice of Mindful Morning and Evening Reflections. Each morning, the practitioner begins by setting a conscious intention for the day, attuning their thoughts and actions to resonate with their manifestation goals. This reflection doesn't need to be long or complex—a brief moment of focused intention while drinking tea or observing nature is often enough. Evening reflections serve as gentle closures to the day, allowing the practitioner to revisit their intentions, recognize any fairy-given signs, and acknowledge progress. These simple, yet profound moments maintain an ongoing connection to the fairy realm, allowing manifestation energy to flow consistently.

The practice of Gratitude and Affirmation Journaling takes this connection further, guided by fairies as a means to root the practitioner's desires within a foundation of gratitude. In a small, dedicated journal, the practitioner records affirmations and expresses gratitude not only for what has already manifested but also for what is yet to come. This gratitude, the fairies teach, acts as a magnet, aligning the practitioner with abundance. It isn't merely a reflection but a powerful tool that transforms expectations into reality. The journal becomes a sacred space, a place where the fairies' energies blend with the practitioner's, holding the intentions close to heart and mind.

Next is the Art of Fairy Chanting and Sound Resonance. Fairy energy is inherently rhythmic, flowing in tones and melodies that echo through the natural world. Sound, they show, is a carrier of intention, and simple, heartfelt chants help amplify and direct manifestation energy. A chant can be a single word or phrase, like "abundance flows" or "peace is here." Spoken with rhythm and repetition, the chant vibrates through the practitioner, bridging intention and energy. Fairies may suggest singing these phrases while in nature, harmonizing with the gentle rustling of leaves or the ripple of water. Through this resonance, the practitioner connects to the natural frequencies, tuning into energies that support their intentions with fairy-guided harmony.

With these practices, the fairies introduce an advanced Visualization Technique for Manifestation Amplification. While earlier visualizations may have focused on a simple, focused image, this technique invites the practitioner to build an entire scenario around their desire, engaging all the senses. If their intention is prosperity, they are encouraged to imagine not just the sight of abundance but the sounds, the textures, and even the scents associated with it. Fairies, whose presence can be both subtle and vibrant, assist by guiding these visualizations, helping the practitioner experience the richness of their desire as if it already exists. Each detail strengthens the vibrational resonance of the intention, weaving it into reality's fabric.

Equally essential is the Practice of Inspired Action, where the fairies gently encourage the practitioner to take steps toward their desires. Manifestation is not only an inward journey but one that requires action, inspired by the connection between intention and life. Fairies often work through gentle nudges and serendipitous signs, prompting the practitioner to take actions aligned with their goals. For instance, if the practitioner seeks connection or community, fairies may inspire them to attend gatherings or engage in conversations that open doors to new relationships. By acting on these prompts, the practitioner shows commitment to their manifestation, grounding their desires in the world of form.

As manifestations begin to unfold, the fairies teach the Practice of Energy Releasing—the subtle art of letting go with trust. This stage of release is akin to a flower blooming in its own time, free of impatience. Fairies, being attuned to nature's cycles, remind the practitioner that manifestation unfolds with its own wisdom. By releasing their grip on how and when a desire will manifest, the practitioner allows the universe and the fairies to work in harmony. This release doesn't diminish focus but rather allows a peaceful, joyful anticipation. Just as fairies trust the cycle of seasons, the practitioner too trusts the cycles of their desires, opening space for unexpected blessings.

Finally, the fairies teach the Ritual of Sacred Celebration, a way to honor manifestations that come to life. Celebration, in the fairy world, is a sacred act, one that strengthens bonds and renews energy. The practitioner is encouraged to pause and honor each step of the journey, whether through a small ceremony or a moment of gratitude. This celebration, however simple, feeds the manifestation cycle, creating a continuous flow of joy, gratitude, and connection with the fairies. In this way, the fairies become not just guides but partners in the practitioner's life, sharing in their joy, and deepening their shared purpose in the mystery of creation.

Chapter 23
Deep Emotional Healing

Beneath the surface of daily consciousness lies a realm where memories, emotions, and energies interweave into the fabric of our being. It is in this silent reservoir that unprocessed emotions, memories, and traumas often dwell, casting shadows over the spirit and affecting one's well-being. Here, the fairies become tender allies, inviting us to release, heal, and ultimately transform these energies. Guided by their presence, we embark on a ritual of deep emotional healing, opening a sacred doorway to profound release and renewal.

The journey begins with Creating a Sacred Healing Space. The fairies reveal that an environment prepared with gentle intention fosters the right energies for emotional release. Select a quiet place, perhaps adorned with flowers, stones, or even a small bowl of clear water to represent clarity. Let natural light or the soft glow of a candle illuminate the space, signaling openness to the fairies. Each chosen element serves a purpose, creating a boundary that nurtures the practitioner's intention to confront and release emotional weight with a compassionate heart.

As the space takes form, the practice of Breath Awareness and Grounding gently draws the practitioner into the present moment. The fairies, attuned to the rhythm of the breath, invite us to follow its natural flow. Slow, mindful breaths calm the mind and body, bridging the conscious world with the inner depths. Visualize roots extending from the base of the spine or feet into the earth, as if grounding into the ancient wisdom of nature itself. This grounding creates a stable foundation, ensuring that even in moments of emotional intensity, the practitioner remains connected to the steady, nurturing energy of the earth and the fairies.

With this grounding established, the fairies guide the practitioner into Emotional Uncovering through Reflection. In this delicate space, they encourage a gentle reflection on feelings or experiences that carry emotional weight. The fairies are sensitive to the vulnerability this exploration brings, offering their calming energy to provide a sense of safety. As memories surface, they may come with an initial wave of emotion—sadness, anger, or even relief. The fairies remind us that each of these emotions is valid, each a part of the healing tapestry, and they encourage us to witness them without judgment.

Next, the ritual deepens with Visualization of Energetic Release. Here, the practitioner envisions these heavy emotions as a tangible mist or color surrounding them, representing the burdens that they are prepared to release. The fairies, often associated with the natural elements, inspire a transformative visualization. Imagine these emotions drifting out into the earth, water, or sky—absorbed and gently dispersed by nature, transmuted back into neutral energy. In this release, the fairies act as intermediaries, ensuring that what is given up is safely and compassionately carried away, returning space for healing light.

An essential part of this process is Acceptance and Self-Compassion, facilitated by the fairies' soft, nurturing presence. Through their gentle energy, the practitioner is reminded to offer themselves kindness, acknowledging the courage required to face their inner shadows. Fairies, ever empathetic, reveal that self-compassion is not only a balm for past hurts but also a vital ingredient for lasting emotional transformation. In the presence of the fairies, the practitioner learns to extend a warm, accepting gaze toward their own journey, no matter how complex or difficult it may have been.

As emotions are released, the fairies introduce the practice of Receptivity to Healing Light. With the emotional space cleared, a new, light-filled energy can enter. Here, the fairies guide a visualization of healing light—a gentle, warm glow that fills the heart and mind. This light may be imagined as golden, silver, or any color that feels comforting, washing over the body like a soothing balm. The practitioner is invited to let this light flow into the spaces once occupied by pain or grief, a soft replenishment offered by the fairies to nurture the renewed spirit.

The ritual closes with Gratitude for the Fairies and the Self. Just as the fairies have given their energy and support, the practitioner takes a moment to thank them for their presence and guidance. This gratitude extends to oneself as well, acknowledging the courage to face and heal deep emotional layers. This ritual of deep emotional healing, guided by the fairies, opens not only the heart but also a path to lighter, freer emotional resonance. As one steps out of the ritual space, they may carry with them a renewed awareness of inner peace, anchored in both the self and in the fairy energy that has embraced them.

The threads of emotion weave a subtle web around the heart, often carrying echoes of past experiences that linger in the present. The fairies, who understand the delicate energies of the unseen, guide us into a deepening of the emotional healing ritual. In their wisdom, they reveal that true release and peace come when we venture courageously into the depths, welcoming emotions as guides toward self-knowledge and inner transformation.

With the groundwork of emotional release established, the fairies introduce the practice of Purifying Breathwork. This gentle, rhythmic breathing invites healing energy with every inhalation and releases tension with every exhalation. As the practitioner breathes, they are encouraged to envision each breath as an infusion of pure, vibrant energy. Slowly, with each cycle, this breath dissolves lingering remnants of sadness, anger, or regret, inviting in a fresh clarity and peace. The fairies, hovering nearby, amplify this breath with their presence, adding a calming rhythm that encourages complete surrender.

In the stillness that follows, the fairies guide the practitioner into the Practice of Emotional Release through

Visualization. Here, images or colors emerge, representing emotions long held within. The fairies reveal that these visualizations offer a path to deeper healing by giving form to feelings that words may not fully capture. Perhaps the practitioner sees a vibrant red for anger, a murky blue for sorrow, or a tangled mass symbolizing confusion. The fairies gently instruct the practitioner to release these colors, allowing each emotion to disperse into the vastness of the earth, sky, or flowing water nearby. Through this act, each emotion is honored and released, returning to the universal flow, transformed by nature itself.

With this release, the fairies guide the practitioner to open their heart to Receiving Light and Love. In this tender space, the fairies themselves, embodiments of compassion and balance, offer their own energy as a radiant light. They invite the practitioner to imagine this light surrounding and filling them, touching every space that was previously occupied by heavier emotions. The practitioner may envision this light as golden or lavender, pulsing with warmth and compassion. Each breath brings this light deeper within, filling the heart, mind, and spirit with a peaceful assurance and gentle empowerment. It is an act of reclaiming one's inner sanctuary, healed and purified.

Next, the fairies lead into a subtle yet profound exercise: Listening for Inner Messages. Emotions, once acknowledged and released, often reveal deeper insights, fragments of wisdom that emerge when the noise of unresolved feelings has dissipated. In the quiet created by the healing ritual, the practitioner may sense a faint whisper within—a newfound clarity, an understanding of their own needs, or a comforting affirmation. The fairies encourage this introspective listening, for they know that within the quiet lies the soul's guidance, a truth that arises only in moments of peace.

As these messages surface, the fairies introduce Affirmations of Renewal and Strength. The practitioner, now attuned to the flow of healing, speaks affirmations that reflect their journey and newfound strength. Statements such as "I release what no longer serves me," "I am open to peace and light," or "I embrace my inner strength" resonate deeply, supported by the fairy energy that surrounds them. Each affirmation anchors the healing, transforming it from a transient experience to a lasting shift within the self. The fairies, perceptive and wise, offer their silent approval, strengthening each word with their subtle energy.

To close the ritual, the fairies suggest a Gratitude Ritual and Offering. Gratitude, they reveal, is a powerful force that enriches the energy exchanged during the ritual, creating a harmonious balance. The practitioner may place a small token—a flower, crystal, or symbol—at the center of their space as an offering to the fairies. This token embodies appreciation for the fairies' presence and guidance, symbolizing the mutual respect between the practitioner and the fairy realm. With this offering, the practitioner acknowledges the fairies' support, grounding the healing within the sacred bond that has been nurtured.

As the ritual draws to a close, the practitioner carries with them a lighter spirit and a heart open to renewal. The fairies, always near yet ever gentle, withdraw their guiding presence, leaving an impression of peace and a whisper of their continued support. Through this deep emotional healing, the practitioner steps forward into life with clarity, resilience, and a profound connection to both their own essence and the tender wisdom of the fairies.

Chapter 24
Working with Elementals

In the mysterious depths of nature, energies exist beyond the realm of fairies, forces that echo ancient rhythms and primal power. These beings, known as elementals, are often mistaken for fairies but carry unique energies and purposes within the natural world. Each elemental spirit reflects one of the foundational elements—earth, water, fire, and air—manifesting their qualities with a raw, almost untamed force that reveals the essence of the element itself.

The journey begins with the Elementals of Earth, beings of grounded strength and ancient knowledge. Known by many names—gnomes, stone spirits, and forest guardians—earth elementals embody resilience and stability. They reside within rocks, soil, trees, and mountains, silently nurturing the roots of all life. When connecting with earth elementals, one is called to embrace the qualities of patience, endurance, and strength. The practitioner may start this connection by spending time in natural landscapes, focusing on grounding practices, and offering small tokens—such as crystals or stones—as gestures of respect and alignment with these grounded energies. In their silent and steady presence, earth elementals impart stability and clarity, supporting us in times when we need to stand firm.

Next come the Elementals of Water, fluid beings that echo the flow and depth of the rivers, lakes, oceans, and even rain. Commonly perceived as water sprites, undines, or nymphs, these spirits dwell in the heart of every wave and ripple, embodying emotions, intuition, and transformation. Water elementals hold the power of change and cleansing, urging the practitioner to let go of emotional burdens and trust in the natural ebb and flow of life. To engage with these beings, one might visit a nearby body of water or create a simple bowl of water as a symbolic connection, watching its surface for subtle movements or reflections that mirror the energy of the undines. Through this connection, water elementals guide us into the depths of our own emotions, helping us embrace vulnerability and fluidity with grace.

Elementals of Fire follow, beings who carry the essence of passion, transformation, and raw energy. Known as salamanders or flame spirits, they are not confined to the physical fire alone but reside in the vitality and warmth of all things, from the sun to the smallest spark. Fire elementals are fierce and potent, guiding practitioners toward courage and personal transformation. To attune to their energy, one might begin with a simple candle flame, focusing on its warmth and flickering movement. Salamanders respond to acts of bravery and intention, offering insights in moments when one seeks to ignite purpose or courage. With their guidance, the practitioner learns to navigate and channel inner strength, transforming obstacles with the same intensity that fire transforms wood into ash.

Finally, there are the Elementals of Air, beings who are as elusive as the wind and as present as every breath. Often appearing as sylphs or wind spirits, these elementals bring qualities of freedom, intellect, and inspiration. They reside in open skies, among clouds, and in each gust of wind, embodying both the stillness and the motion of thought. When seeking to work with air elementals, one might observe the patterns of clouds, feel the wind's touch on the skin, or simply focus on breathing deeply, inviting their light and clarity. Sylphs respond to our desire for openness and knowledge, guiding us in moments of mental clarity and creative thought. Their presence is like a gentle breeze that clears away mental fog, encouraging the practitioner to see with clarity and a broadened perspective.

As these elemental beings are encountered, practitioners find that each embodies not only the qualities of their element but also the deeper mysteries of existence. Earth elementals teach the wisdom of roots and persistence, water elementals reveal the healing within surrender, fire elementals awaken transformation, and air elementals inspire freedom and understanding. Working with these spirits requires respect and attentiveness, as elementals resonate with the core energies of life itself, powerful and unaffected by human desires.

The practice of working with elementals is not about control but about building a relationship of mutual respect and reverence. They are not summoned or commanded but instead honored as allies in personal and spiritual growth. When approached with humility, these beings share their profound insights and energies, offering guidance and empowerment in a way that is deeply personal and transformative. The fairies, too, recognize these elemental spirits as kin, understanding that each carries an essence vital to the balance of all things.

Through this first exploration, practitioners begin to sense the distinct presence of these elemental allies. Each holds a unique voice, a resonance that calls out in specific times of need or growth. As we deepen our connection with the elementals, they remind us that we are part of a vast and interconnected web of existence, where the forces of earth, water, fire, and air come together to sustain and transform all life.

Once a practitioner has formed an initial connection with earth, water, fire, and air elementals, a new depth of interaction becomes possible—one that transcends simple observation and enters the realm of spiritual co-creation. This deeper relationship invites a resonance between human and elemental energies, fostering a balanced and reciprocal exchange. As one aligns with the spirits of nature, rituals and practices emerge that both honor these beings and enhance the practitioner's connection to the elemental forces that guide and sustain life itself.

To begin this journey, the practitioner may consider creating a sacred space specifically designed for working with elementals. This space, whether indoors or outdoors, serves as a point of connection, a threshold where the energies of each element can freely manifest and be honored. A clearing in a natural landscape may work as well as an altar adorned with symbols of each element: crystals or soil for earth, water in a glass bowl, a lit candle for fire, and incense or feathers representing air. Such a space aligns one's intentions with the elements, allowing a harmonious environment for engaging with elemental spirits. When entering this space, the practitioner centers themselves, inviting each elemental presence to be felt, establishing an atmosphere of respect and receptivity.

A more active communication with elementals unfolds naturally in these settings. Earth elementals, for example, may signal their presence through a heightened sense of stability or a grounded feeling that spreads through one's body. Practitioners can enhance this interaction through physical grounding exercises, touching the earth, or simply breathing deeply, allowing themselves to become as rooted as the trees. With water elementals, one may feel waves of calm or emotional openness; this energy can be cultivated by holding water in one's hands or watching its movement, consciously attuning to the element's rhythm and openness.

For those drawn to fire elementals, entering a deep connection means invoking a sense of inner strength and transformation. Here, one might sit before a candle flame, envisioning it as a bridge to the salamanders, feeling the energy of warmth and courage stirring within. Such rituals not only honor fire elementals but awaken the practitioner's own potential to rise and transform in moments of challenge. Meanwhile, working with air elementals may involve meditative breathing exercises or focusing on the feel of wind or breath against the skin, experiencing air's ephemeral clarity and inviting insight. Sylphs often manifest as fleeting ideas or a sudden clarity, a reminder that inspiration and knowledge are as fluid as the wind itself.

With time, practitioners begin to develop elemental rituals—practices unique to their connection with each spirit. These rituals are less about formal steps and more about an intuitive alignment with the element's energy. An earth ritual may involve the act of planting a seed with intentions of growth and grounding, allowing the spirit of earth to nurture both the seed and the practitioner's goals. Water rituals could involve washing one's hands in a stream or ocean, allowing the water to cleanse and carry away unneeded emotions or energies, a ritual in which water elementals aid emotional clarity and release.

Fire elementals inspire rituals of transformation. One might write limiting beliefs on paper and burn it in a small flame, symbolizing a release and transformation of these energies with the guidance of salamanders. Air elementals, similarly, inspire rituals of release and renewal. Whispering intentions or wishes into the wind, allowing it to carry one's words and energy, creates a subtle but profound bond with the sylphs. Each elemental ritual, personal and deeply intentional, becomes an opportunity for partnership with the elemental realm, blending human consciousness with the wisdom of nature's forces.

Beyond individual rituals, elementals guide practitioners toward a more profound awareness of natural cycles and their interplay. Earth's grounding energy intensifies in spring, a season of planting and growth; water's flow is strongest during times of rain and in transitional seasons, bringing emotional renewal; fire's potency rises in summer, a time for action and transformation; and air's clarity peaks in autumn, offering inspiration and insight as nature prepares for rest. These cycles mirror the rhythms within, and elementals become allies in recognizing and harmonizing with these energies, teaching us to live in balance.

Finally, as practitioners integrate elemental practices into their lives, a sense of co-creation emerges. Working with elementals is not a matter of control but a collaborative dance where the practitioner's intentions blend with the natural forces, enhancing rituals and fostering growth. Earth teaches patience and endurance, water imparts adaptability, fire brings courage, and air gifts perspective. These spirits remind us that life is a constant interaction with forces beyond our control, yet by honoring these forces, we find harmony.

In this deepened relationship, practitioners gain not only insight but a felt sense of unity with the world. Elementals, ancient and wise, offer themselves as guides, teaching us the rhythm of nature and our place within its vast, interconnected web. And as this connection strengthens, so too does the practitioner's ability to work with the elemental forces in ways that honor both the spirit and the sacred elements that shape all existence.

Chapter 25
Deep Purification Ritual

The act of purification has long stood as one of humanity's most profound and sacred rites, an offering of oneself to the energies of renewal, a willing release of all that weighs upon the soul and spirit. In the context of elemental magic and fairy connections, purification serves as both an invitation and a clearing of pathways. It aligns the practitioner with clarity, free from energies and emotions that cloud perception and connection. As fairies embody nature's purity and vibrancy, entering their presence through ritual cleansing deepens the bond, welcoming their influence and guidance.

Preparing for a purification ritual requires deliberate intent and an environment free from distraction. The space chosen should resonate with calm and stillness—ideally a place near nature where earth, water, fire, and air converge. This location might be a clearing in a forest, a secluded garden, or a quiet streambed. If practiced indoors, the altar or ritual space should include symbols for each element, grounding the setting in a natural harmony. Here, herbs, crystals, and flowers can amplify the purity sought. Common choices include sage or rosemary for earth, salt water for cleansing, a candle flame for transmutation, and incense for clarity of air.

In preparation, the practitioner centers themselves, entering a place of deep awareness. Breathing deeply, they consciously begin to release surface tensions, visualizing any restless energies dissipating with each exhalation. In this moment, they stand on the threshold, a bridge between the weight of the past and the promise of lightness to come. When invoking fairies, it is crucial to honor their natural affinity for purity, as their energies are closely aligned with nature's balance and clarity.

The ritual of purification often begins with the element of earth. With bare hands, the practitioner may sprinkle a handful of salt or place stones around their feet, drawing on earth's grounding force. This symbolic grounding strengthens the intention to release all energies that no longer serve. While holding the salt or stones, one can silently express gratitude to earth elementals, asking for their assistance in anchoring stability through the cleansing. Fairies connected to the earth may offer their presence subtly—a feeling of warmth or an inner calmness, guiding the practitioner's intent toward centeredness.

Next, water becomes the medium of release, reflecting its power to cleanse the spirit as it washes over the body and soul. Dipping one's hands into a bowl of water or, if outdoors, using the fresh water from a nearby stream, the practitioner envisions negative energies and stagnant emotions flowing into the water. This practice symbolizes release, aided by water elementals that carry away residual negativity. The practitioner may choose to sprinkle the water upon themselves or trace circles with dampened fingers on the skin, each motion a prayer of renewal. Invoking fairies of water, one may feel a softening, a gentleness, as if emotions long held begin to dissolve, leaving behind a sense of lightness.

The ritual then embraces the energy of fire, symbolizing transformation and the purification of deeper, unseen aspects of self. A single flame, whether from a candle or a small fire, becomes the focal point, embodying the spirit of transformation. Here, the practitioner holds a piece of parchment, a leaf, or any natural symbol that represents what they wish to release—be it fear, self-doubt, or a past hurt. Gently offering it to the flame, they observe as it is consumed, transformed into smoke and ash. This act is accompanied by a sense of liberation, a tangible release supported by fire elementals, who bring warmth and courage. Fairies aligned with fire carry this intention upwards, whispering resilience into the heart of the practitioner.

Finally, the element of air completes the ritual. Incense or smudge smoke fills the space, rising and swirling, reaching into all corners of the aura. The practitioner may walk through the smoke, moving their hands through it, feeling its lightness as it drifts, lifting away any last fragments of heaviness. As air touches the skin, it brings clarity, a sense of openness, like a window thrown wide to the morning light. Air elementals, present in the whirls of smoke or a breeze that may arise, help clear the mental fog, offering insight and heightened perception as the ritual closes.

With the completion of each elemental phase, the practitioner rests, eyes closed, feeling the cumulative effect of the ritual. A natural sense of peace arises, along with an impression of having shed an invisible weight. The fairies' energies, subtle yet palpable, seem to linger, blessing this act of self-cleansing. Each element has played its part, balancing and refreshing the practitioner's aura, opening pathways to deeper connection and harmony with the world of fairies.

To conclude, a word of gratitude is offered, silently or aloud, honoring each elemental force and the fairies that have accompanied this process. In giving thanks, the practitioner acknowledges the transformation achieved, recognizing it as part of an ongoing journey, a cyclical return to clarity and inner harmony.

This purification ritual invites fairies to remain near, sensing the purity of intention and the alignment of the practitioner's spirit with the elemental realms. It is a rite of self-renewal, an act of reverence for the interconnectedness of human and elemental energy, reaffirming one's place within the vast dance of nature. As the practitioner steps away from the ritual, they carry with them a renewed aura, clear and receptive, open to the teachings and presence of the fairies that inhabit the world around them.

In the aftermath of a profound purification ritual, subtle shifts often begin to unfold, as if the essence of each element has imprinted upon the practitioner's spirit, amplifying inner clarity. This second layer of purification beckons the practitioner to dive even deeper into the ritual's energy, transcending the visible forms of each element to reach the unseen threads that connect the self to the greater whole. Here, the ritual of purification becomes a journey into the soul, an invitation to engage with the fairies' energies on a level where vibrations harmonize and clarity sharpens, moving through layers of the aura and beyond.

As preparation for this advanced stage, the practitioner settles into a meditative space, grounding and centering once more. A soft resonance grows as the fairies begin to draw near, their energies blending with the subtle pulse of each element present. Each of these forces — earth, water, fire, and air — serves not only as a foundation but as a living bridge, carrying the practitioner beyond surface purification to an enduring state of energetic renewal.

The ritual commences with a chant or incantation, a rhythmical invocation whispered or sung to honor the elemental fairies and to deepen alignment with the energies present. Each word is chosen with care, drawing from the language of the heart, as if speaking directly to the fairies, inviting their wisdom and guidance. The practitioner allows their voice to soften and resonate, creating a vibration that clears away the remnants of prior energies and invites purification into deeper spaces of the spirit. The rhythm of the chant, combined with breath, forms a delicate dance, awakening inner vibrations that resonate with the fairies, guiding them closer.

To magnify this connection, light visualizations become central. In this stage, the practitioner envisions their aura as a field of soft, radiant light that gently expands and flows. Beginning at the feet, light rises, gradually filling each part of the body and spiraling around it, shifting from a soft glow to a brilliant, encompassing sphere. Within this aura, visualizations of each element appear in turn — a deep earthen green, a flowing blue, a warm orange, and an ethereal white. These colors intermingle, symbolizing the unity of elements within and around, an embodiment of balanced energy.

While immersed in this visualization, fairies connected to each element may make their presence known, weaving through these colors, enhancing the visualized energy field with their vibrations. Earth fairies strengthen the foundation of this sphere, imbuing it with stability, as if grounding every corner of the mind and spirit. Water fairies flow through in gentle currents, purifying emotions and washing away unseen residues. Fire fairies add sparks of transformation, encouraging courage and the release of old patterns, while air fairies whisper clarity, allowing the mind to clear, guiding the practitioner toward spiritual insight.

As the aura becomes brighter and more balanced, the practitioner extends their arms, feeling the weight of purification deepen into the soul. At this stage, the ritual may include a sacred offering to the elements, symbolic tokens of appreciation for their energies. This offering could be in the form of flower petals, grains, or small crystals, each corresponding to an element. As these offerings are placed on the ground, they connect with each element, becoming vessels through which gratitude and intention are expressed. Fairies gather around these offerings, accepting them as symbols of reverence and respect, and, in turn, magnifying the energies present in the ritual space.

The practitioner's focus then shifts to breathing techniques designed to carry the purification process further into the depths of the subconscious. They inhale slowly, feeling the clean energy of each element filling their lungs, and exhale to release any lingering tension, a steady rhythm cleansing from the core outward. With each breath, the practitioner visualizes layers of inner resistance dissolving, gradually uncovering a pure, receptive state, ready to embrace the energies of the fairies fully.

After several minutes of mindful breathing, the final phase of the ritual calls for closing gestures. The practitioner slowly brings their hands to the heart, acknowledging the presence of the fairies and expressing silent gratitude for their guidance. Hands extend outward, palms facing the earth, releasing all residual energy into the ground, where it will be absorbed, transmuted, and renewed by the elemental forces. This grounding action serves as both a release and a closing, a return to the natural cycle.

As the practitioner concludes, they might notice a lightness within, a feeling that echoes the vibrancy of the fairies. This purification ritual, now complete, leaves a quiet, profound clarity—a soul refreshed and attuned to the quiet whispers of nature. The fairies' presence lingers, woven into the aura, creating a bridge between realms and leaving the practitioner with an unmistakable sense of connection and clarity that will accompany them forward.

Purification through the fairies and elements is not merely a ritual act; it is an alignment, a restoration of the self within the larger natural order, opening paths for deeper engagement and spiritual insight in the days to come.

Chapter 26
Developing Intuition

The development of intuition often begins as a gentle stirring within, a quiet sense that surpasses the ordinary, guiding individuals to insights often unseen by the rational mind. For those who seek to align with fairy energy, intuition becomes more than an inner whisper; it is a vibrant connection with the subtleties of the natural world, a doorway into realms alive with wisdom and wonder.

The first steps toward developing intuition are marked by practices of inner attunement. Fairy energies are delicate, woven into the very fabric of the earth's rhythms, and sensing them requires a mind and heart that are clear, calm, and receptive. To begin, one might start with daily mindfulness exercises, grounding the senses in each moment's texture. Practicing awareness of one's breath or observing the rise and fall of thoughts without attachment gradually attunes the mind, creating a space in which intuition can flourish.

Mindfulness also extends into the physical world, where nature observation practices become a sacred exercise. Whether sitting beneath a tree, watching the gentle sway of leaves, or feeling the texture of soil between one's fingers, these moments become pathways for noticing subtle changes in energy. Fairies, as beings of nature, resonate with this grounded presence and respond to it, often imparting delicate impressions to those who are observant. Noticing how a breeze changes or how certain sounds emerge and dissipate can offer hints of fairy presence, gentle nudges from realms unseen.

The process of inner attunement also deepens through specific breathing techniques aimed at enhancing sensitivity.

Fairy energy flows in waves, often light and subtle, and the breath can be used to draw this energy inward. Through deep, rhythmic inhalations and slow exhalations, practitioners encourage their energy fields to synchronize with these vibrations, opening gateways of perception that go beyond the physical. The act of breathing becomes a bridge, a way to bring oneself closer to fairy frequencies and to soften the edges of conscious thought.

As intuition awakens through these practices, symbolic meditation becomes a key to refining it further. Symbols serve as focal points, tools that fairies often use to communicate across realms. For instance, the practitioner might choose a natural symbol, such as a leaf or a stone, and hold it during meditation, exploring its textures, weight, and patterns. The symbol becomes an anchor, a conduit for energy, helping focus the mind and guiding the intuitive senses toward subtler messages that fairies often leave in symbolic form.

While meditation deepens one's awareness, the use of crystals offers another dimension in developing intuitive abilities. Crystals like amethyst, clear quartz, and moonstone are known to heighten intuition, resonating with the energy of the third eye chakra, which governs inner vision. The practitioner may place a crystal over the brow or hold it during meditation, inviting it to amplify inner perceptions. Fairies, who are drawn to the energies of the natural world, often align their presence with such objects, subtly amplifying the crystal's effect to assist the practitioner in accessing inner knowledge.

As intuitive senses strengthen, practicing energy scanning introduces a more hands-on approach. With eyes closed, the practitioner moves their hands over objects or within specific spaces, allowing the palms to sense energy variations. This practice sharpens the ability to recognize warmth, coolness, or tingling sensations, which often signify areas rich in fairy energy. Each scanning session allows the practitioner to notice even the smallest shifts, creating a foundation for recognizing fairy presence and the nuanced energies they bring forth.

In time, intuitive perception is further honed through journaling insights and reflections. This process serves as a way to document patterns, symbols, and experiences that may seem isolated but reveal their meaning over time. Each entry, no matter how brief, becomes a record of insights received, dreams that hint at fairy messages, or even symbols that appear in everyday life. Over time, patterns emerge, offering clarity and building confidence in the messages the practitioner perceives.

With growing intuition, the practitioner's journey with fairies transforms, unveiling an enriched dimension of their presence.

As the intuitive senses continue to open and reveal layers of hidden understanding, the journey deepens into the intricate art of distinguishing true intuition from the countless thoughts that often arise in the mind. For those working with fairies, clarity of intuition becomes paramount, for these beings speak in ways that bypass logic, weaving messages into the natural world and into one's inner landscape. The cultivation of discernment and attunement now becomes a guiding force, enabling practitioners to trust the authenticity of what they sense and feel.

One of the first steps in refining intuition is developing the ability to differentiate between intuitive insight and rational thought. Intuition, unlike logical reasoning, often presents itself in spontaneous ways, emerging as a soft but distinct feeling, an image, or an unshakable sense of knowing. To practice this, the practitioner may spend time in meditation, observing thoughts as they come and go without attachment, like leaves carried by a gentle stream. This detachment trains the mind to release habitual thinking patterns, allowing true intuition to arise naturally and with unmistakable clarity.

Further enhancing this discernment, visualization exercises deepen the mind's receptivity to messages from fairies. Visualization serves as a bridge between the physical and etheric worlds, preparing the mind to accept subtle impressions with greater detail and accuracy. One effective technique is the "garden visualization," where the practitioner imagines entering a vibrant natural setting, calling upon the presence of fairies, and allowing them to communicate through imagery, colors, or even symbolic elements that appear in this mental space. By refining this practice, the practitioner becomes adept at recognizing the authenticity of these impressions and discerning their meanings.

To support the subtlety of these practices, specific crystals continue to play a crucial role. Stones like celestite and labradorite are known to resonate with the ethereal and intuitive realms, encouraging clarity and connection to unseen energies. When placed on the third eye or held during meditation, these crystals amplify intuitive perception and align one's energy with the delicate vibrations that fairies naturally emit. Their presence acts as a gentle amplifier, helping separate genuine insights from mental noise and heightening the ability to detect fairy messages in the subtlest forms.

As intuition becomes more responsive, the practitioner might explore dreamwork as another medium for fairy communication. Fairies often choose to communicate during sleep, a time when the conscious mind rests and the unconscious becomes more accessible. Before sleep, the practitioner can set the intention to connect with fairy energies, perhaps placing a crystal by the bed or keeping a symbolic item nearby. In the dream state, fairies may appear as guides, symbols, or even as nature itself. Upon waking, journaling these experiences without analysis keeps the impressions intact, allowing their meaning to unfold naturally over time.

For those deeply immersed in this intuitive journey, learning to sense and interpret energy shifts in natural settings becomes an advanced skill. When walking through a forest, meadow, or near a stream, the practitioner can pause and tune in to changes in the air or sensations in the body. A soft tingle, a feeling of warmth, or a sudden sense of lightness often signals the presence of fairies. With practice, the practitioner learns to interpret these energetic shifts, discerning which impressions are genuinely from the fairy realm and which may be reflections of their own thoughts or emotions.

To further strengthen and protect intuitive receptivity, the use of energetic shielding techniques provides a safeguard for clear communication. Fairies, being beings of pure and light-filled energy, respond to and respect boundaries. By visualizing a soft, radiant light surrounding the body, the practitioner establishes a safe space, filtering out energies that do not resonate with their highest intentions. This shield not only fosters clarity but creates a sacred space where the fairies' messages can flow freely and be received with trust.

Finally, to anchor these practices, the ritual of intuitive gratitude becomes a powerful method for grounding and honoring this deepening connection. After each intuitive experience or communication with fairies, a quiet moment of thanks acknowledges their presence and the insights gained. This gratitude ritual is simple yet profound—perhaps a silent affirmation, the offering of a flower, or a few words spoken to the earth. This closing ritual brings a gentle conclusion to each session, harmonizing one's energy with that of the fairies and weaving the bond of intuition ever more closely with the natural and mystical world.

Through these practices, intuition transforms from a mere sense into a profound connection, allowing the practitioner to walk with fairies not just in rituals but in the very essence of daily life.

Chapter 27
Harmony in Relationships

As the connection with fairies deepens, a new chapter opens, inviting their gentle energy into the intricate web of human relationships. Fairies, with their harmonious attunement to the natural world, bring invaluable insights into restoring balance and empathy within relationships, revealing the unseen energy exchanges that occur between individuals. Embracing this wisdom allows the practitioner to foster understanding, compassion, and genuine com
nection with others—a sacred aspect of spiritual growth.

A fundamental step in creating harmony is preparing a space dedicated to nurturing positive energies in relationships. Just as the earth, water, fire, and air fairies hold specific roles within the elemental balance of nature, each relationship thrives when certain energies align and flow harmoniously. To begin, the practitioner may choose a serene location, indoors or outdoors, where calming elements can be introduced: soft lighting, crystals that evoke peace and connection (such as rose quartz and green aventurine), and the gentle scent of herbs like lavender or chamomile. This space serves as a sanctuary, a place to focus on healing and strengthening the bonds with loved ones.

In this sacred setting, the practitioner can perform the Fairy Ritual for Empathy, a practice that invites fairies to assist in deepening understanding and fostering compassion. With a quieted mind and open heart, they call upon fairies of the water element—known for their sensitivity and emotional depth—to aid in dissolving barriers and misunderstandings that may have formed. Holding a symbol of the relationship, whether it's a small token or a photograph, the practitioner sets the intention for empathy and understanding to flow freely, imagining the fairies' gentle energy enveloping this intention. In their presence, the practitioner may feel a renewed ability to see from the other's perspective, gaining insight into their emotions and motivations.

Alongside empathy, patience is an essential quality that fairies can help cultivate within relationships. Earth fairies, with their grounding and steadfast nature, embody patience as they nurture and sustain life around them. Inspired by their energy, the practitioner may invoke earth fairies in moments of tension or conflict, asking for the strength to respond with calm and composure. A quiet affirmation repeated silently—such as "I am grounded in peace"—serves to root this intention, channeling the fairy's steadfast patience and wisdom into the heart, fostering a calm that allows understanding to flourish over time.

As emotional layers are explored, the practice of forgiveness becomes a potent path to harmonizing relationships. Fairies, who move freely between the seen and unseen worlds, offer their guidance in releasing burdens that weigh heavily upon the heart. By setting a gentle candle alight and invoking air fairies—masters of movement and release—the practitioner visualizes tensions and grievances dissipating like mist carried away by a breeze. This ritual need not be dramatic; it can be a soft and silent expression of the desire to let go, clearing space within for renewed trust and peace. Through the fairies' influence, forgiveness becomes an act of liberation, allowing emotional renewal and balance.

To further cultivate harmony, the ritual of compassionate communication is introduced, inviting fairies to help guide words and emotions. Often, misunderstandings arise not from intention but from the energy carried within one's words. By invoking fairies of the fire element—symbolic of passion and expression—one may find that their words become infused with warmth and clarity. As the practitioner speaks, they may envision a soft, amber light around their words, which carries their intentions of kindness and honesty. This mindful practice aligns the heart and voice, helping to dissolve tension and bring a sincere quality to all exchanges.

Another ritual known as heart-centered breathing draws on the power of air fairies to restore harmony between oneself and others. Here, the practitioner sits quietly, envisioning the presence of these gentle beings surrounding them. As they breathe in, they imagine drawing in a light, airy energy that fills the heart with warmth and peace. Each exhalation releases any lingering resentment or frustration, offering it to the air fairies who transform it into lightness. With each breath, a sense of calm and connection deepens, creating a state of receptivity that extends naturally to others, bridging gaps that may have formed in the relationship.

For those relationships that may require a more consistent or ongoing nurturing, the fairy charm of friendship can serve as a tangible reminder of intention. This charm can be as simple as a small stone or token infused with the practitioner's desire for harmony, trust, or connection. By holding the charm and calling upon fairies of unity and friendship, the practitioner imbues it with this wish. Kept in a place of prominence, it becomes a symbol of the fairies' ongoing support, carrying the energy of friendship into the heart of the relationship.

Through these gentle rituals and practices, a bond with fairies becomes a bridge to understanding and empathy in all relationships. The fairy world teaches that harmony is not a static state, but a flowing, living balance—one that requires attentiveness, compassion, and an open heart, each quality enhanced by their timeless, supportive presence.

As the practitioner becomes attuned to the fairies' influence in relationships, they begin to witness subtle shifts—moments where previously tense exchanges soften, where misunderstandings unravel effortlessly. This is where the energy of compassionate communication finds its deeper expression, supported by the fairies' guidance. To sustain this harmony, the practitioner learns to go beyond simple ritual; they discover the art of nurturing the bond continually, allowing fairy energy to become a quiet but present force in their exchanges with loved ones.

One way to strengthen this ongoing connection is through the practice of energetic attunement, which involves recognizing and adjusting to the fluctuating emotional states of those close to us. Here, the practitioner may call upon air fairies, whose sensitivity to movement and unseen currents makes them ideal allies in this endeavor. In a quiet moment, the practitioner closes their eyes, visualizing their loved one enveloped in a soft, pale light that sways and shifts, revealing any subtle tensions or emotional currents. As they breathe in, they draw this energy into their own awareness, acknowledging it with empathy and understanding. With each exhalation, they release a steadying energy back into the visualization, offering calm and acceptance. This act of energetic exchange becomes a grounding force, creating a harmonious resonance that extends naturally into their interactions.

To deepen this harmony, the ritual of grounding in shared spaces provides an opportunity for both individuals to unite their energies with the support of fairies. Earth fairies, with their enduring presence and connection to the soil, offer a model of steadfast harmony. In a chosen area—a garden, a quiet room, or even a shared meditation spot—the practitioner and their loved one may sit together, holding a stone or small crystal that represents their connection. By visualizing roots extending from this object into the earth, they link their intentions for harmony and understanding, grounding them in the stable and nurturing energy of the earth fairies. This simple ritual can transform the space into a place of refuge, a reminder of their commitment to compassion and balance, even when they face challenges.

The fairies also impart a unique awareness of energy blockages that may hinder harmony. Fire fairies, known for their transformative power, become instrumental here, guiding the practitioner through a gentle, symbolic cleansing of emotional blockages. With the presence of fire fairies invoked, the practitioner visualizes a small flame within their own heart or the heart of their loved one. This flame, bright yet soft, illuminates any lingering fears, resentments, or unresolved hurts, allowing these to rise to the surface. As the flame grows warmer, it begins to dissolve these blockages, replacing them with a sense of openness and vulnerability. Through this gentle, fairy-guided transformation, relationships are gradually cleansed of old emotional scars, creating space for renewed trust and intimacy.

Another advanced practice introduced by the fairies involves mirroring rituals, which allow individuals to reflect each other's energies and deepen their empathy. Water fairies, with their fluid nature and natural reflective qualities, support this practice. In a quiet setting, the practitioner imagines themselves as a still pond, receptive and open to the emotions of their loved one. As they meditate on this image, any emotions, expressions, or energies from their partner flow across their mind like ripples on water. With the support of the water fairies, the practitioner begins to understand these reflections, intuitively grasping the underlying emotions behind words and actions. This ritual, though subtle, fosters a profound empathy that can lead to greater harmony and a more profound understanding of each other's experiences.

To ensure these practices are integrated naturally into daily life, the fairies introduce symbolic objects into the practitioner's routines, each representing a quality they wish to nurture in their relationships. These can be as simple as a small branch to symbolize flexibility, a stone for stability, or a feather for gentle communication. Each object, consecrated with the guidance of fairies, serves as a gentle reminder of the qualities needed to maintain balance and compassion. Whenever tensions arise, the practitioner may hold or look upon these objects, reconnecting with their intentions and the fairies' ever-present support.

Finally, as they deepen their journey with the fairies, the practitioner comes to recognize that maintaining harmony requires consistent personal reflection and renewal. Fairies remind us that relationships mirror our inner states, and therefore, self-awareness and emotional clarity are crucial. Through a practice of weekly reflection, supported by earth and water fairies, the practitioner contemplates their actions, words, and emotions over the past days. By offering gratitude for moments of understanding and committing to improve any areas where tension arose, they create a space of accountability and self-compassion. This reflection, conducted under the gentle guidance of fairies, becomes a balm that soothes and nurtures, ensuring that the energy of harmony continues to flourish.

In weaving these practices together, the practitioner becomes a vessel of fairy-inspired compassion and empathy, able to bring light and understanding into each relationship. The fairies, in their timeless wisdom, reveal that true harmony in relationships is a living process—one that grows stronger through dedication, empathy, and a deep connection to the magical, unseen energies that surround us.

Chapter 28 Deepening Practice

The journey of deepening one's practice begins with the act of consistent, mindful meditation. Rather than a structured or guided meditation, the fairies encourage a softer, more open approach—one that mirrors the undulating rhythms of nature. Each day, the practitioner finds a quiet space, whether a secluded glade or a simple corner adorned with natural items, and allows themselves to settle into a receptive state. In these moments, no agenda is set; instead, the practitioner remains open, listening to the subtle messages of the fairies. Often, this quiet communion allows the energies of nature to reveal their presence through sensations, images, or soft intuitions. Over time, these meditative practices deepen, evolving into a form of intuitive communication where the fairies' guidance feels as natural as a gentle breeze or the warmth of sunlight.

In parallel, the fairies introduce the concept of cyclical dedication—an acknowledgment of nature's cycles and seasons, mirrored in the practitioner's own development. By setting intentions aligned with lunar phases or seasonal shifts, the practitioner learns to harmonize their personal growth with the greater rhythms of life around them. During the new moon, for instance, they may focus on setting new intentions, asking the fairies for support in manifesting qualities such as patience, compassion, or resilience. As the moon waxes, these intentions are nurtured, gradually gaining strength, until they reach fruition during the full moon, when the fairies' energies are at their peak. In this way, the practitioner's dedication to growth is not a rigid path but one that ebbs and flows, allowing for natural cycles of reflection and renewal.

Integral to this deepening practice is the keeping of a spiritual journal, a living record of the journey. Within its pages, the practitioner captures moments of connection, insights, and the soft, often hidden wisdom that fairies impart. This journal becomes a cherished tool for reflection, a mirror of the practitioner's progress and evolving relationship with the fairies. By documenting these subtle exchanges, they can observe patterns over time, noting how certain fairy messages recur or how their own perceptions deepen with each season. As the years pass, the journal becomes a map, guiding them through past discoveries and reminding them of the paths they have traversed—a testimony to their commitment and growth.

Alongside these reflective practices, the fairies encourage rituals of renewal, which cleanse and recalibrate the practitioner's energy. Much like a spring rain that washes the forest, these rituals serve to clear accumulated doubts, distractions, or emotional weights that may hinder the connection with the fairy realm. Using water fairies as guides, the practitioner may choose to perform a symbolic cleansing under the moonlight or with a handful of blessed herbs steeped in water. With each drop, they imagine cleansing their spirit, allowing any energies that no longer serve them to be carried away. By integrating such rituals, the practitioner learns the art of self-renewal, maintaining a clear, vibrant connection to the energies that sustain their journey.

The fairies, in their timeless wisdom, also impart the importance of observing one's progress without judgment. As the practitioner deepens their practice, they become aware of moments when their connection feels strong and others when it may seem faint or distant. Instead of frustration, the fairies encourage the practitioner to approach these fluctuations with compassion and curiosity, viewing each experience as part of a greater cycle. In times when the connection feels tenuous, the practitioner may seek the grounding energies of earth fairies, who offer a comforting presence and remind them of the steadfast nature of their path.

To ensure the continuity of growth, the fairies reveal a practice called anchoring moments, in which the practitioner consciously marks their milestones. These anchors are small rituals of gratitude—simple acts that reinforce the progress made and honor the bond with the fairies. For instance, after a year of dedicated practice, the practitioner might plant a tree, consecrating it as a living emblem of their journey and dedication. With each new leaf and branch, this tree mirrors their growth, serving as both a reminder of their commitment and a beacon of the fairy energies that support them.

As the chapter draws to its natural close, the fairies impart one final piece of wisdom: the path of continuous expansion. With each practice, each meditation, and each season, the practitioner's spirit unfurls, much like a fern in morning light. The relationship with the fairies becomes a river of endless possibilities, and though the practitioner has journeyed far, the fairies reveal that there is no true end to this path. It is a path where growth is continuous, where new wisdom is forever waiting, and where each day, each breath, brings the practitioner closer to the heart of the fairy realm and the mysteries it holds.

As the journey of spiritual practice unfolds, the path deepens, weaving itself through the practitioner's daily life in ways both subtle and profound. The fairies, ever-present and vigilant, guide this process with gentle hands, revealing the art of inner refinement and the grace of expanding self-awareness. In this stage, the practitioner is invited to embrace not only the connection with fairies but to live in harmony with their teachings—a life steeped in sensitivity to the energies around and within.

At the heart of deepening this connection is the practice of daily consecration. Each morning or evening, the practitioner dedicates a few moments to realigning with the intentions set in the earlier stages of practice. By lighting a candle, saying a brief invocation, or simply closing their eyes in silence, they affirm the commitment they have made—not as an obligation, but as a gesture of love and respect toward the fairies and the energies that guide them. Over time, these brief yet profound moments of consecration become as familiar and nourishing as breaths, drawing the practitioner ever deeper into a state of constant presence and gratitude.

The fairies, ever inclined toward nature's flow, introduce a unique perspective on adaptation and flexibility in spiritual practice. They encourage the practitioner to learn the rhythm of their own spiritual tides, recognizing when to delve into intense meditation and ritual and when to embrace periods of quiet reflection. During times of heightened energy or enthusiasm, the practitioner might feel drawn to engage in more elaborate rituals or prolonged communion with the fairies. At other times, the fairies advise the practitioner to rest, to let the waters settle, allowing insights and energies to flow without resistance. Through this rhythm, the practitioner becomes attuned to the natural cycles within, mirroring the ebb and flow of nature's seasons, and deepening their understanding of balance.

One of the most profound lessons shared by the fairies in this stage is the practice of silent observance. By observing nature without the need to interact or interpret, the practitioner becomes a witness, an open vessel through which subtle fairy energies flow. This silent observance is a meditation in itself—a way to watch a stream move, to listen to wind passing through leaves, or to gaze at a moonlit sky. In these moments, the practitioner's energy becomes still, resonating with the elemental presence of the fairies. Over time, these practices open an intuitive awareness, allowing the practitioner to receive insights and messages beyond the realm of words, deepening their communion with the invisible forces that surround them.

As the practitioner becomes more adept at weaving fairy energies into everyday life, the fairies introduce the concept of personalized ritual creation. Here, they invite the practitioner to rely less on structured ritual forms and more on their own intuitive insights to create rituals that resonate deeply. These rituals may be simple or elaborate, yet they always reflect the practitioner's unique relationship with the fairy realm. Whether it involves creating an offering of flowers by a stream, writing a poem of gratitude, or whispering intentions to the wind, these rituals are a form of living art—a dance between the practitioner's soul and the fairy energies. With each new ritual, the practitioner reinforces their bond, expressing devotion not through routine but through creativity and genuine presence.

Integral to this deepening practice is the guidance to develop a personal sanctuary—a sacred space within the practitioner's home or garden, dedicated solely to communion with the fairies. Unlike an altar, this sanctuary is a larger, more immersive environment where the practitioner can retreat whenever they seek clarity, peace, or renewal. This space might include objects found in nature, symbols of the elements, or anything that feels connected to the fairy energies. Here, the practitioner cultivates a sense of belonging, knowing that this sanctuary exists as a tangible manifestation of their connection to the fairies. Over time, the energies within this space grow potent, infused with the fairy essence, becoming a haven where the practitioner can meditate, reflect, or simply be in the presence of these mystical beings.

The fairies also introduce a profound practice called harmonizing with inner seasons. Just as nature has its cycles, so too does the soul. During moments of introspection, the practitioner is encouraged to reflect upon which "inner season" they are experiencing. If in a "spring" phase, the practitioner might feel inspired to set new intentions or learn new practices, as fresh energy blooms within them. In "summer," they may feel vibrant, actively engaging with their rituals and connections. During "autumn," a phase of release, they may find it's time to let go of habits or attachments that no longer serve their path. Finally, in "winter," a time of rest and inner stillness, the fairies advise the practitioner to withdraw and conserve their energy, nurturing the seeds of future growth. By tuning into these inner seasons, the practitioner aligns their spiritual journey with a natural and gentle progression, creating harmony between their inner and outer worlds.

This phase of spiritual deepening reaches its essence in the practice of perpetual gratitude. Here, the practitioner learns to infuse every moment, from the smallest gesture to the most profound ritual, with a sense of appreciation for the energies, beings, and experiences that shape their path. The fairies, whose presence is woven into every aspect of life, become active participants in this gratitude practice, receiving the energy of appreciation and amplifying it. Through this practice, the practitioner realizes that gratitude is a powerful tool—not only for maintaining harmony with the fairies but for fostering a profound state of joy and fulfillment within. Gratitude, when practiced as a constant state, becomes a light that illuminates the path forward, ensuring that every step taken is imbued with reverence and respect.

With these practices, the practitioner finds that their connection to the fairies has transcended the boundaries of formal rituals or defined spaces. It becomes a living relationship, one that breathes, grows, and evolves continuously. The fairies, ever watchful and nurturing, have shared their wisdom generously, guiding the practitioner to a place of self-reliance, where the knowledge of fairy energies is no longer external but embedded within the practitioner's spirit.

Thus, the journey of deepening practice is one of continuous expansion, a quiet and steady merging of self with the forces of nature and spirit. And as this connection matures, the practitioner finds that they no longer seek the fairies as separate beings, but recognize them as an inseparable part of their own essence—a journey that continues to unfold, moment by moment, season by season.

Chapter 29 Ancestry and Fairies

In the deepest, most hidden corners of ancient forests and in the hushed whispers of mountain peaks, there lie memories of those who have walked this earth before us. These memories, interwoven with the fabric of nature itself, linger in rocks, trees, and streams, carrying whispers of past lives, dreams, joys, and sorrows. Guardians of this ancient knowledge, the fairies embody the living memory of nature, binding the past to the present and serving as stewards of ancestral wisdom that spans centuries. Their presence invites us to see beyond the surface of things, to sense the threads that connect us to those who lived long before, and to realize that our lives are part of an unbroken chain stretching back through the ages.

This lineage is not simply a record of names, dates, and family histories but an energy that pulses within us, shaping our strengths, struggles, dreams, and even our deepest fears. The fairies, in their boundless wisdom, help us understand ancestry as something alive—a stream of consciousness and spirit that flows into our own being. They remind us that, like trees intertwining their roots to share nutrients and communicate, we are linked to our ancestors in ways that go beyond words. Every heartbeat we feel echoes with the rhythms of those who came before, and by tuning into this resonance, we can access a wisdom and strength that surpasses our immediate understanding.

The fairies guide us into this awareness with a delicate and patient touch, encouraging us to look at ancestry as a tapestry of experiences woven into the energy of our souls. Through their guidance, we learn to recognize that the invisible threads of our lineage influence not only who we are but who we have the potential to become. Yet, this connection to the past requires cultivation—a willingness to look inward, to explore the depths of our own roots. Engaging in rituals that honor those who walked before us, we begin to experience their presence as part of our everyday lives. Simple offerings left in nature—a scattering of grains, a handful of wildflowers, or a stone placed carefully by a stream—become acts of remembrance, a way of inviting our ancestors to walk with us once more.

These rituals, although seemingly small, possess a profound symbolism. In leaving these tokens in natural spaces, we create a bridge between our world and that of our ancestors. The fairies, serving as intermediaries between realms, ensure that these gestures are received and understood, honoring both our lineage and the mystical forces that connect us to it. They understand that these offerings are not mere tokens but profound acknowledgments of a past that lives within us. The fairies, with their innate sensitivity to the flow of energies, guide these gestures to resonate through time, allowing us to feel that our ancestors are indeed close, even as they remain unseen.

Among the practices that open doors to our ancestors, ancestral meditation is one of the most transformative. Here, the fairies encourage practitioners to find a quiet, secluded place in nature—perhaps beside an ancient tree or a secluded grove—to begin their journey within. Sitting in silence, we allow ourselves to feel the land beneath us, to breathe in the air that nourished our ancestors, and to open our hearts to the energies that surround us. The fairies help us visualize roots growing from our bodies into the earth, intertwining with the roots of our ancestors. These roots extend deep into the soil, reaching beyond the limits of time and space, creating a network of support and wisdom that sustains us.

This practice is far more than a meditation; it is a form of communion with the essence of our heritage. Each time we reach out to these roots, we reconnect with the spirit of those who shaped the path we walk today. The fairies, in their gentle way, help us access this energy, guiding us toward a sense of belonging that is as ancient as the mountains and as enduring as the rivers. Through this connection, we begin to sense the presence of ancestors within us as living influences, each heartbeat carrying forward their wisdom, their dreams, and their love.

Another layer of this journey involves ancestral stories, which serve as a vital means of rekindling our connection to lineage. Even when family records have faded or specific memories have been lost to time, the fairies encourage us to explore the general heritage and cultural symbols that resonate with our ancestry. They inspire us to rekindle this connection by delving into folklore, traditional rituals, and the tales passed down through generations. In honoring these stories—whether gathered around a fire, beneath a starlit sky, or in the solitude of a forest clearing—we open ourselves to the truths embedded within them. The fairies, who bear witness to these recitations, create a space where the energies of these stories can awaken, filling us with insights and a sense of belonging.

As we listen to these tales, we may find ourselves tapping into the dreams and struggles of our ancestors, experiencing their joys and sorrows as if they were our own. The fairies act as quiet guardians of these moments, helping us recognize the relevance of these stories in our own lives. They reveal that these tales are more than mere history; they are messages, carrying guidance, warnings, and lessons meant to aid us in our own journeys. This rekindling of ancestral stories becomes a ritual of remembrance, a way to honor the dreams and sacrifices of those who paved the way for us.

Dreamwork is another pathway through which fairies help us connect to our ancestry. With their natural affinity for liminal spaces, the fairies guide us into a state of openness before sleep, allowing ancestral energies to visit us in dreams. By setting an intention to connect with ancestors before drifting into slumber, we create a bridge to the world of spirit, where messages from the past can emerge. In these dreams, guided by the fairies, we might receive messages, images, or symbols that offer wisdom or insight. Over time, with patience and practice, our ability to recall and interpret these dreams sharpens, allowing us to uncover the patterns and wisdom woven into our spirits by those who came before us.

The fairies guide us to approach each dream with reverence, encouraging us to keep a journal and record the details, symbols, and emotions that surface. Through this practice, we start to perceive connections that might otherwise be missed, patterns that reflect the experiences and insights of our lineage. In the world of dreams, our ancestors become more than distant figures; they are companions, offering guidance, comfort, and the occasional glimpse into our shared past. With each message, each symbol, the fairies help us see that our ancestry is not a mere memory but a living force, one that walks with us every day, even in the realm of dreams.

A further and deeply sacred practice is the creation of an ancestral altar. This dedicated space serves as a focal point for connection with lineage, honoring both the known and the unknown members of our family tree. On this altar, we might place items that hold personal or cultural significance—photographs of loved ones, stones or soil from ancestral lands, symbols of our heritage, or even heirlooms passed down through generations. The fairies, who serve as guardians of this altar, ensure that the energies remain harmonious and inviting, providing a comforting presence that fills the space. As we light candles, leave small offerings, or simply pause to reflect, we invite our ancestors into our lives, creating a sacred bond that defies the constraints of time.

These altars are not just physical spaces; they are gateways to the spirit world. By tending to these altars, we make our respect tangible, our gestures imbued with love and acknowledgment. Each time we approach the altar, we reinforce the bond that ties us to our heritage, drawing strength from those who walked the earth before us. The fairies encourage us to keep this space alive with offerings, whether it be a flower, a token, or a heartfelt message, each an act of reverence that affirms our place in the lineage of souls. The altar serves as a constant reminder that we are not alone, for we carry the presence of our ancestors with us always.

One of the most profound aspects of this journey lies in ancestral forgiveness and healing. The fairies, with their gentle wisdom, help us recognize that within every lineage, there may be unresolved pains or lingering burdens passed down through generations. These energies, which may manifest as personal challenges or patterns in our lives, are echoes of past traumas, fears, or conflicts that were never resolved. Through meditative practices, the fairies guide us to visualize these burdens as energies that can be acknowledged, released, and transformed.

The process of ancestral healing becomes a journey of compassion, where we extend forgiveness to those who may have struggled, erred, or suffered in ways that affected future generations. The fairies, acting as intermediaries, facilitate this release, allowing us to let go of what no longer serves, clearing the way for peace and harmony to flow through the ancestral line. With each act of healing, we contribute to a legacy of love and understanding, transforming our lineage in ways that resonate through time.

As we deepen our relationship with ancestry, our understanding of heritage expands to include not only individual ancestors but the broader spirit of humanity. The fairies, ever-present guides, introduce us to symbols and customs that speak to the collective heritage we share with others. Each cultural symbol or ancestral custom becomes a means of accessing the energies tied to our ancestral lands, a conduit through which we connect with the broader tapestry of human experience. Wearing these symbols or incorporating them into rituals fills our practice with the energy of those who walked similar paths, reminding us of the universal connections that bind us all.

With the guidance of the fairies, seasonal offerings become rituals that honor the cyclical nature of life and death, echoing the natural rhythms that our ancestors once revered. In spring, flowers and young plants honor the renewal of life; in autumn, grains and roots celebrate the harvest. Each season is infused with its own ancestral memories, reflecting the lives and experiences of those who adapted to the changing cycles of the earth. Through these rituals, we acknowledge that our connection to heritage flows not only backward through time but also outward to encompass the universal experience of life on earth.

Chants and songs provide yet another means of connecting to our collective ancestry. The fairies encourage us to discover traditional melodies, whether passed down through family or inspired by the lands of our forebears. Each word and note resonates through time, summoning the energy of countless voices that sang these tunes before us. As we sing, we may feel the presence of those who came before, their spirits joining in a chorus that bridges generations. The fairies, amplifying this energy, help us sense the collective power of our lineage, a force that transcends the boundaries of time and space.

Finally, practitioners are guided by the fairies to embark on a pilgrimage—whether physical or in spirit—to the places tied to their roots. Envisioning these lands becomes a sacred act, a way of stepping into the landscapes our ancestors once knew. If it is possible to visit these places, each step taken there becomes a prayer, a gesture of reverence for the land that once nourished those who came before. But even if the journey remains within the mind's eye, the fairies help us feel the essence of those lands, allowing us to walk the paths of our ancestors in spirit.

The culmination of this journey is a ceremony called the Ritual of Ancestral Communion, where practitioners gather items that represent both past and present—soil, candles, traditional foods—and perform a sacred ritual that invites ancestral energies into their lives. This ritual, often held under open skies or in the presence of trees, becomes a space where the fairies, the ancestors, and the practitioner come together in a communion that celebrates the bonds of lineage. In this moment, practitioners feel the blessing of every life that has come before them, interwoven into their own spirit.

By the journey's end, we stand not as isolated individuals but as bearers of a legacy, guardians of memories, wisdom, and love that span beyond our own lives. The fairies, who have walked with us through each ritual and meditation, reveal the beauty of living in harmony with our roots. They show us that the weight of the past need not be a burden but a source of endless strength, one that connects us to the timeless essence of nature and spirit. And in this communion, we discover that we are a part of an endless chain, a link that holds all of nature, humanity, and spirit together in a timeless embrace.

Chapter 30
Self-Healing Ritual

In the gentle twilight where the everyday world meets the realm of spirit, fairies bring forth their innate ability to heal, inviting practitioners into the sacred art of self-healing.

The self-healing ritual unfolds as an intimate dialogue with the self, guided by fairies who understand the energetic imbalances that often manifest as physical or emotional discomfort. In their presence, practitioners are encouraged to acknowledge the pain they carry—whether visible or hidden. Fairies offer a nonjudgmental space, urging practitioners to approach their pain with the same compassion they might extend to others. This approach transforms the self-healing ritual into a powerful act of self-compassion, where the practitioner learns to embrace and transmute their own energies.

Fairies introduce practitioners to the art of energetic cleansing, a vital first step to self-healing. Through visualization and deep breathing, practitioners learn to release stagnant energy from their body, allowing fresh, vibrant energy to flow freely. Fairies guide them to imagine a gentle stream of light coursing through each part of their body, washing away blockages, doubts, or fears. This cleansing process feels like a spring rain clearing the air, refreshing the spirit and preparing the practitioner for deeper healing. With each breath, practitioners can feel layers of tension dissolve, as though the fairies were sweeping away cobwebs from their inner world.

At this stage, practitioners are encouraged to connect with healing crystals and herbs that fairies cherish. By incorporating specific crystals like rose quartz or amethyst and plants such as lavender or chamomile, practitioners create an environment where healing energies resonate powerfully. These natural allies are more than mere tools; they become energetic companions, each chosen with the guidance of fairies for their unique properties. Fairies reveal that when these items are mindfully placed within a healing space or held close during meditation, they amplify intentions, creating a gentle but potent synergy of energies that promotes physical and emotional recovery.

With the energy cleansed and the space prepared, fairies invite practitioners into guided visualization journeys designed to foster self-healing. Through these journeys, practitioners enter an inner landscape shaped by their unique needs and memories. Fairies lead them to places in nature—a quiet forest glade, a peaceful riverbank, or a luminous cave—where they can immerse themselves in restorative energies. In these sacred spaces, fairies encourage practitioners to sit quietly, feeling their presence, and allowing the energies of these imagined sanctuaries to envelop and heal them. Each breath taken in this space acts as an elixir, filling them with a profound sense of safety and calm, far removed from the anxieties of everyday life.

In this safe space, fairies introduce practitioners to the power of affirmations for self-love and healing. These words are not simple phrases but carriers of intention, each carefully selected to resonate with the practitioner's core. The fairies encourage them to speak phrases like, "I am whole," "I am resilient," or "I am worthy of peace," while focusing on areas of tension or pain within the body. With the fairies' guidance, these affirmations become vibrant with healing energy, weaving themselves into the practitioner's spirit. Each word spoken is like a drop of light, filling spaces where wounds or doubts may have lingered, and instilling the practitioner with a new sense of empowerment and inner harmony.

In moments of deep vulnerability, fairies teach practitioners to use self-embrace as a healing gesture. This involves placing hands over the heart or gently holding one's shoulders, embodying a sense of presence and care for the self. Fairies reveal that this simple act connects the practitioner's physical and emotional bodies, grounding them in the here and now, and opening them to a compassionate exchange of energy with themselves. In these embraces, practitioners feel as though the fairies themselves are wrapping them in wings of light, whispering encouragement and support.

For practitioners facing more intense or persistent emotional wounds, the fairies introduce a ritual of self-forgiveness. With their gentle guidance, practitioners are encouraged to acknowledge past experiences that have left lingering effects on their spirit. Fairies illuminate that true healing often involves releasing guilt, shame, or self-blame, allowing practitioners to reclaim aspects of themselves lost to past pain. This ritual is performed by lighting a candle as a symbol of clarity and rebirth, while silently offering forgiveness to themselves, as if healing an old wound. As the candle burns, practitioners feel the weight of these memories lifting, replaced by a sense of lightness and freedom, as though they are becoming more themselves with each moment.

In closing the self-healing ritual, fairies guide practitioners into grounding practices that anchor their restored energy within the physical body. This final step involves focusing on the sensations in their feet, imagining roots extending deep into the earth, connecting them to the solidity and stability of the ground below. Through this visualization, fairies ensure that the healing energy gathered during the ritual is sealed within, woven into the fabric of the practitioner's being. Grounded and renewed, practitioners emerge from the ritual with a sense of wholeness, deeply aware of their innate capacity for healing and self-love.

Once practitioners have embarked on the journey of self-healing, they enter a sacred realm where personal energy harmonizes with the nurturing presence of fairies. In this second phase, the healing ritual deepens, evolving into an experience of profound regeneration and inner transformation. Fairies guide the practitioner to explore new dimensions within themselves, where healing extends beyond immediate relief to a lasting, rooted state of well-being. Every breath, every gesture becomes a testament to the potential for renewal that lies within the spirit.

In the heart of this ritual, the fairies introduce the art of guided breathing to amplify the flow of healing energy. Practitioners are encouraged to synchronize their breath with the rhythm of the earth, inhaling deeply and exhaling with intention. The fairies direct each breath to different parts of the body where healing is needed, carrying with it an invisible current of strength and release. With every inhale, practitioners draw in light, calm, and resilience; with each exhale, they let go of tension, doubts, and past grievances. Fairies emphasize that this breathing is not simply a mechanical process but an act of communion with the life force that animates all of creation. Each breath becomes a bridge, connecting the practitioner to both their inner self and the surrounding world.

Building upon this, the fairies guide practitioners into visualization exercises to strengthen the mind-body connection. They introduce the imagery of gentle, glowing light—pulsing softly at the center of the body, expanding outward with each breath. This light radiates healing energy, traveling to areas of discomfort or stagnation, flooding them with warmth and vitality. Fairies encourage practitioners to perceive this light as a representation of their own innate healing power, which grows brighter and more radiant with focused intention. This visualization not only soothes but also empowers, inviting practitioners to witness their own capacity to generate and direct healing forces from within.

In this journey, fairies also introduce the concept of color therapy as a means of enhancing the emotional depth of the ritual. They explain that each color embodies a distinct frequency and offers unique healing properties. Guided by fairies, practitioners learn to envision colors that resonate with their needs, enveloping themselves in hues that soothe, energize, or uplift. A golden light may wrap them in comfort and protection, while a blue or green glow might calm the mind and restore peace. Fairies invite practitioners to experiment, trusting their intuition to choose colors that align with their intentions. This exploration of color not only enhances the ritual's effectiveness but also deepens the practitioner's sensitivity to subtle energies and emotions.

Throughout the ritual, fairies emphasize the importance of affirmative touch, a practice where practitioners gently place their hands over areas of tension or pain. This touch, infused with healing intention, brings attention and awareness to parts of the body that may feel disconnected. Fairies suggest that practitioners combine this touch with affirmations, creating a powerful union of physical and energetic healing. With each touch and affirmation, practitioners cultivate a sense of compassion and acceptance for their body, viewing it not as a separate entity but as a sacred vessel that deserves respect and care.

As the ritual progresses, fairies encourage practitioners to explore the realm of energetic sound. Soft humming, vocal tones, or even listening to natural sounds, like the rustle of leaves or gentle rain, become integral to the healing journey. Fairies reveal that sound carries vibrations capable of reaching deep layers of the psyche, unlocking blocked energies and emotions. Practitioners are invited to hum or chant in a way that feels natural, tuning their voices to resonate with their bodies. Fairies gently guide this process, helping practitioners discover tones that correspond to each part of their body, activating healing energies within. This practice transforms sound into a sacred healing instrument, amplifying the power of the ritual and harmonizing the practitioner's internal frequencies.

Toward the close of the ritual, fairies introduce gratitude as a transformative practice. Here, practitioners are invited to pause, acknowledging the journey they have taken through their inner landscape. Fairies suggest expressing gratitude not only for the healing received but also for the strength within that allowed them to undertake this journey. They encourage practitioners to offer thanks to their own spirit, for its resilience, and to the fairies for their guidance and support. This act of gratitude, simple yet profound, anchors the healing energies within the practitioner's being, strengthening the bond between their spirit and the forces of nature.

In the final moments, fairies guide practitioners in a ritual of closure, a practice that seals and preserves the healing energies awakened during the ritual. Fairies encourage practitioners to visualize a protective, shimmering aura around themselves, a gentle barrier that maintains the newfound balance within. This aura, a blend of light and intention, is an energetic reminder that healing is an ongoing state, protected and nurtured over time. Practitioners are reminded that this aura not only holds the energies cultivated in the ritual but also acts as a shield against external negativity, ensuring that their inner peace remains intact as they return to the world beyond the ritual space.

Emerging from the ritual, practitioners carry with them the essence of the fairies' wisdom. The self-healing process is not merely about alleviating discomfort but about cultivating a lifelong relationship with one's own spirit, body, and emotions. Practitioners leave with the understanding that their connection with fairies is not limited to moments of ritual; instead, it is an ongoing companionship, present in each breath, each moment of self-care, and every act of kindness toward themselves. The fairies' teachings continue to resonate, guiding practitioners toward a life marked by balance, resilience, and a profound respect for their own journey.

Chapter 31
Final Consecration

As the journey of transformation draws near its end, the fairies prepare practitioners for a sacred moment of consecration, where all their learning, healing, and growth is gathered into a single act of dedication. This consecration ritual is not merely ceremonial; it is a profound recognition of the bond forged between the practitioner and the fairy realms, an acknowledgment of the path traveled, and an honoring of the intentions that carried them through. The fairies guide practitioners to create a sacred space, a threshold where the tangible and ethereal worlds meet, where they will consecrate the symbols and objects representing their journey.

At the heart of this consecration ritual lies the creation of a dedicated sacred space. Fairies instruct practitioners to choose a place where they feel a natural sense of calm and connection, a location that resonates with the presence of nature—be it a quiet corner, a garden, or a special room. They guide the practitioner to cleanse this area with elements that honor the earth, using dried herbs or fragrant resins to purify and sanctify the space. Practitioners are encouraged to move slowly, allowing the smoke or scent to drift through the air, honoring the space and inviting the energies of protection and support.

In this consecrated space, the practitioner is then guided to assemble an altar of intention. Each object chosen for this altar becomes a vessel for memory and intention, representing different aspects of the journey they have undertaken. Fairies suggest including items that hold personal significance, such as crystals, feathers, leaves, or stones that remind the practitioner of key moments, symbols of protection, healing, or transformation.

These objects are not only representations of the path traveled but also act as conduits of energy, grounding the ritual and strengthening the connection between realms. Each item is gently placed with a mindful intention, allowing the altar to emerge as a living reflection of the practitioner's experiences, hopes, and inner growth.

Once the altar is arranged, fairies guide practitioners to initiate the first phase of consecration through a personal dedication ritual. In this ritual, the practitioner is invited to speak words of dedication, affirming their intentions and acknowledging the bond they have developed with the fairies and their spiritual practice. The words are not scripted; instead, fairies encourage practitioners to speak from the heart, trusting that sincerity will carry the energy of their dedication. This act of spoken dedication solidifies the commitment, weaving the practitioner's intention into the energy of the space and the objects around them. Each word becomes a thread, binding together the symbols of the altar, the energies of the ritual, and the spirit of the practitioner.

In a profound act of alignment, the fairies then introduce the use of natural elements in the consecration, allowing earth, water, fire, and air to bless the objects on the altar. Practitioners are guided to place a small vessel of earth or a crystal representing the grounding power of the earth, a bowl of water for emotional clarity, a candle to embody the transformative power of fire, and a feather or incense smoke to honor the breath of air. Each element is introduced with intention, allowing its energy to infuse the altar and each object. Through these elements, practitioners honor the natural forces that have accompanied them throughout their journey, invoking them to seal and protect the sacred space.

The ritual continues as practitioners enter into a moment of silent reflection and communion, guided by the fairies to connect deeply with the energies present. In this silence, the fairies reveal their presence subtly, through a gentle sense of calm, a light breeze, or an inner warmth that seems to rise from the heart. This is a time for practitioners to listen, receiving any final messages or impressions from the fairy realm. Fairies encourage practitioners to remain open, allowing memories, insights, or even symbols to arise, honoring these as a final gift from the journey. This silent reflection becomes a space of integration, where all that has been learned and experienced is allowed to settle, to take root within the practitioner's spirit.

After this communion, the fairies guide practitioners to bless and consecrate a personal object or symbol that represents their spiritual journey. This object, chosen with care, may be a crystal, pendant, or a small token from nature—something that can be kept close as a reminder of the sacred journey. Holding this object, the practitioner is guided to visualize the energies of the ritual, the altar, and the elements converging within it, imbuing it with protection, guidance, and the wisdom of the fairies. This consecration transforms the object into a talisman, an anchor for the practitioner's spiritual growth, embodying the bond they have cultivated and the lessons they carry forward.

As the ritual draws to its close, the fairies introduce a final gesture of release and gratitude, inviting the practitioner to offer a symbolic gift back to nature. This gift may be a flower, a handful of seeds, or a small natural offering, given as a token of respect and appreciation for the energies and guidance received. Fairies encourage practitioners to bury or place this offering outdoors, in a space where it will become part of the earth once more. This act of giving back is a quiet, humble gesture, acknowledging the cycle of reciprocity and reminding practitioners that they are part of a larger, living web of connection.

In this final consecration, the practitioner steps into a space of spiritual alignment and completion. The altar, now charged with intentions and the energies of the elements, becomes a sacred point of reference, a place of renewal they can return to whenever they seek guidance or strength. The personal object, now consecrated, serves as a tangible reminder of the fairies' teachings, a symbol of resilience and transformation. And in their heart, the practitioner carries a deep sense of gratitude and peace, knowing that their journey with the fairies is an eternal bond, one that will continue to support and inspire them beyond the pages of this book.

As the final consecration unfolds, the ritual invites practitioners to move beyond the tangible altar and into the deeper layers of their own spirit, sealing the commitments, transformations, and newfound connections in a profound energetic bond. In this moment, fairies guide practitioners toward a final act of closure, a reverent merging of realms, where their journey's essence is honored with both silence and celebration.

At the heart of this completion lies a ceremony of gratitude. The fairies encourage practitioners to reflect on the journey that has led them here, to each lesson, ritual, and connection that has woven itself into their being. Gratitude, they remind, is a force of pure alchemy, a vibration that harmonizes energies and resonates deeply with the fairy realm. Practitioners are guided to quietly speak words of thanks to the earth, to the fairies, and to the natural elements that have accompanied them on this path. As each word is spoken, a silent acknowledgment resonates, forming an invisible thread of unity between them and the unseen forces that have become allies in spirit. In this gratitude, practitioners find themselves softened, reminded of the grace that flows from nature when approached with reverence and humility.

As the ceremony continues, practitioners are guided to release intentions into the universe, letting go of specific outcomes and surrendering their journey to the natural flow of life. The fairies remind them that while each ritual and connection has carried a purpose, true spiritual alignment is found in allowing things to unfold organically. This act of release, subtle yet powerful, symbolizes a trust in the journey ahead, a trust in the wisdom they have gained, and a trust in the fairies' presence as a continuous, unseen force. Practitioners are encouraged to visualize their intentions rising like seeds carried on a gentle wind, trusting that they will take root where they are most needed.

In this space of completion, practitioners are guided to close the ritual with a grounding gesture, reconnecting themselves with the earth. This grounding is not just physical but serves as an energetic seal, anchoring the ritual's energy and integrating it fully into the practitioner's being. Fairies suggest a simple act, such as placing hands on the earth, feeling the solidity beneath them, and allowing any residual energy to flow into the ground. This grounding reminds practitioners of their place within the natural world, a tangible connection to the life force that sustains all and binds them eternally to the fairy realm.

With this grounding, practitioners enter a moment of inner silence and stillness, an invitation to reflect on the journey completed and to listen, one final time, for the subtle impressions of the fairies. Here, in this stillness, is the moment where the transformation truly integrates, not in the form of spoken words or active rituals, but as a quiet knowing that rests deep within. In this silence, practitioners may feel a sense of closure, as if an invisible chapter has turned. The fairies are felt, not through movement or sound, but as a gentle, enduring presence—like a soft breeze or a delicate fragrance that lingers as they take their leave, retreating back into nature's hidden folds.

This final consecration ritual also includes a symbolic act of rebirth, a reminder that each step along this journey has transformed practitioners from within. They are guided to breathe deeply, inhaling the freshness of the air, the essence of renewal. In this breath, practitioners are invited to feel the clarity of each lesson, the strength of each connection, and the wisdom they now carry. With each exhale, they release old energies, patterns, and fears, embodying the growth they have embraced. This breath, simple yet intentional, symbolizes their rebirth as beings forever touched by the fairy realm, grounded in nature yet open to the mystical wonders it holds.

As the ceremony draws to a close, practitioners are led to offer a blessing for the future—for their path ahead, for the world, and for the preservation of the fairy realms. This blessing is a gentle wish, a heartfelt intention that fairies hold close, a wish for harmony between all beings, visible and unseen. In this final blessing, practitioners acknowledge the cycle of reciprocity, understanding that their connection with fairies is an eternal exchange. They are encouraged to hold this blessing in their heart, to let it be a guiding light, and to carry forward the spirit of this journey in every encounter, every thought, and every act of kindness they share with the world.

In the final moments, the fairies impart a message of ongoing support and presence, a reassurance that while this formal journey may conclude, the connection remains alive, accessible in the gentle touch of the wind, the vibrant colors of dawn, and the whispers of trees. This parting message is a reminder that practitioners are never alone, that the fairies, now companions of spirit, will walk quietly beside them, guiding, protecting, and inspiring from beyond the veil of the seen world. And as practitioners take their first steps beyond this ceremony, they carry with them a sense of unity, a kinship with the earth, a timeless connection with the fairy realm, and a heart forever touched by the mysteries that lie within nature's embrace.

Epilogue

As you reach the end of this journey, you are not leaving a story behind. Instead, you are carrying with you the essence of this universe of mysteries and revelations, a quiet and subtle legacy that is now part of who you are. This book, which began as a simple reading, has transformed into an experience, a silent initiation into the world of fairies and elements. You have glimpsed the forces that maintain balance and harmony in nature, and now, those forces live within you, transforming you, awakening you to life with new eyes.

What you have learned throughout these pages does not dissolve with the end of the reading. The teachings of fairies, their link with the elements, now resonate within your own being. Walk with this wisdom, allowing each step to reflect the balance you found when connecting with the earth, water, fire, and air. This wisdom does not dwell in words but in the feelings that were stirred, in the expanded perceptions. You have become part of this cosmic dance of energy, a dance that pulses in every leaf, every drop, every breeze, and every flame.

As you live this integration, you realize that fairies are more than mere guardians; they are spiritual allies, reflecting the potential for transformation we all carry within. By honoring them, you also honor yourself, as each element mirrors the deepest facets of your own being. The earth fairies remind you of your resilience and stability; the water fairies, of the fluidity and adaptability within you; the fire fairies, of your passion and drive to create and transform; and the air fairies, of your freedom and ability to see beyond the immediate.

This book has shown you that connecting with nature is more than observation—it is a commitment, a way of life in tune with the universal rhythm. Now, it is up to you to nurture this bond, to stay attuned to the energies around you, to understand that everything is interconnected and that each thought, each action, can reverberate in the cosmos. May you continue to cultivate this respect for the unseen, for it is not only magical but essential for the harmony of the world we live in.

This end is merely a new beginning, for the true magic of what has been learned lies in daily practice, in the willingness to see the beauty and mystery in the ordinary. May you continue this journey with an open heart, with a soul willing to embrace the extraordinary within the simple. Fairies will always be present, in the small details, in moments of stillness, reminding you that the world is far vaster and deeper than our senses can capture.

Now, every experience, every challenge, can be seen as part of this eternal cycle of growth and renewal. At your core, you carry the certainty that you are part of something grand and harmonious. So, as you close this book, remember that the true essence of magic is the connection with life itself and that the enchantment of the world of fairies does not end here—it extends to each choice, each new discovery, each breath. And may this dance between you and the universe continue, forever, in perfect and mysterious harmony.

www.ingramcontent.com/pod-product-compliance
Lightning Source LLC
LaVergne TN
LVHW040141080526
838202LV00042B/2988